D1087101

The Aims of Phenomenology

The Aims of Phenomenology

The Motives, Methods, and Impact
of Husserl's Thought

Marvin Farber

HARPER TORCHBOOKS ❧ *The Academy Library*
Harper & Row, Publishers, New York

To the memory

of

Edmund Husserl

Designed by Darlene Starr Carbone

Contents

Preface

The present book is intended to serve as a critical introduction to phenomenology. It is based upon the author's studies as recorded in the literature over a period of many years. They include the monograph, *Phenomenology as a Method and as a Philosophical Discipline* (University of Buffalo Publications in Philosophy, 1928), "A Review of Recent Phenomenological Literature" (*Journal of Philosophy*, 1930), "Professor Driesch on Philosophical Modes of Procedure" (*Journal of Philosophy*, 1932), "Husserl's Cartesian Meditations" (*Philosophical Review*, 1935), and the author's contributions to *Philosophical Essays in Memory of Edmund Husserl* (edited by M. Farber, Harvard University Press, 1940) and to *Philosophy and Phenomenological Research*. The second chapter is largely reprinted from the Husserl memorial volume of 1940. A brief portion of the third chapter and the main part of the sixth chapter are reprinted with some changes from the monograph of 1928. In addition, materials from surveys of phenomenology and existentialism prepared by the author for a Unesco project have been included. They help to show the nature and extent of the influence of Husserl's thought, with developments certainly far removed from his own ideal of philosophic inquiry. The last two chapters of the present work give an indication of his influence on avowedly phenomenological writers, and also upon many who have become known as existentialists. They record the upsurge of a new literature that has now become more extensive than ever.

Despite the span of time, the author's point of view has

remained fundamentally the same, and his initial differences with one of the honored masters of his youth have been maintained in principle; for it is a complete philosophy that is at stake. But, first of all, it is necessary to give a fair hearing to the teachings and aims of the great phenomenologist. No serious student or reader of philosophical literature can afford to ignore those teachings, which represent a high point of an important section of the tradition of philosophy.

The present writer's books on *The Foundation of Phenomenology* (second edition, Paine-Whitman, 1962), *Naturalism and Subjectivism* (Charles C. Thomas, 1959), and the forthcoming book on *Phenomenology and Existence* (Harper and Row) provide additional studies of the nature and reaches of phenomenology.

Marvin Farber

Buffalo, New York
August, 1966

I

Edmund Husserl and the Aims of Phenomenology

A. Edmund Husserl and the Foundation of Phenomenology

It is always a hazardous undertaking to attempt to decide which recent or contemporary thinkers may be candidates for membership in the "great tradition" of the history of philosophy. There is good reason to suppose that Edmund Husserl, who was professor of philosophy in Freiburg, Germany, will have earned that distinction, along with such recent philosophers as James, Dewey, and Whitehead. "Phenomenology" has come to be generally known as referring to Husserl's philosophy, despite Hegel's use of the term. Husserl's usage was historically independent of that of Hegel. Like Hegel, he inherited from the great tradition in philosophy, and he was inclined to view his predecessors as either adumbrating or falling short of his own ideas. But his principle of selection was different, since he began with the theory of knowledge rather than with metaphysics. That he might well have been compelled by the requirements of a universal idealistic philosophy to move in Hegel's direction is plausible, and is in fact suggested by some of his later writings.

1

The name of Edmund Husserl has become a familiar one in recent world philosophy. He is known as the most vigorous critic of the prevailing "psychologistic" philosophies at the close of the nineteenth century. That he was also an opponent of naturalistic or materialistic philosophy, and that he derived much of his motivation from that opposition, is less generally recognized. He is also known as one of the forerunners of the *Gestalt* psychology; as a profound and fruitful worker in the field of logical theory; as a painstaking descriptive investigator of the structures of experience and its objects; as a champion of the ideal of a rigorous science of philosophy; as a continuator of the idealistic tradition in philosophy; as an effective teacher, with influence on scholars in such different fields of thought as law, psychiatry, mathematics, religion, sociology, and psychology, as well as in philosophy; as one of the conspicuous influences on the development of existentialism; and as the point of departure of the International Phenomenological Society, which was founded in New York one year after Husserl's death in 1938. Certainly Husserl was one of the most seminal philosophical minds in the last century, and he is sure to be intensively studied and critically discussed in the coming generations. It would not be surprising to find a special version of phenomenology ultimately defended as the last stronghold of idealism, or adapted for the purposes of a religious philosophy, in opposition to the philosophical movements motivated and conditioned by the special sciences.

Edmund Husserl was born in Czechoslovakia in 1859, and studied in Berlin and Vienna. He was trained in mathematics, in which field he took his doctor's degree, and also in physics, astronomy, and philosophy. At the suggestion of his friend Masaryk, who was later the president of Czechoslovakia, Husserl attended the lectures of the Catholic philosopher, Franz Brentano, in Vienna. It was Brentano who convinced him of the value and dignity of philosophy as a lifework; and it was through Brentano that he made contact with the tradition of medieval philosophy, and received the first impetus that led to the development of an independent science of phenomenology.

Husserl has left a revealing tribute to Brentano,[1] to whom he always acknowledged indebtedness. His own resemblance to his teacher with respect to the seriousness of his purpose, the whole-hearted devotion to his task, regarding philosophy as a "life or death matter," the absence of humor as a device to enliven lectures or to help score a point, the fatherly treatment of faithful students, and the insistence upon agreement and fidelity; these are traits that must be familiar to all who knew either Brentano or Husserl. Also similar was the apparent inability (which was really in large part disinclination) to understand a novel point of view. Thus Husserl, upon meeting Brentano in later years, found it impossible to convince his old master that he had something radically new to contribute to philosophical thought. But Husserl himself developed the tendency to remain solidly within his own framework of ideas, motives, and definitions. The isolated independence with which he maintained his "inner view" in later years was reminiscent of a Liebnizian monad, with its absence of doors and windows.

Like Kant, Husserl was a slowly maturing thinker. He was past forty years old when he completed his *Logical Investigations* (1900–1901), and fifty-four when his *Ideas Toward a Phenomenological Philosophy* appeared (1913), a work which marked the development of his transcendental philosophy. His first published work, the *Philosophy of Arithmetic*, appeared in 1891. This work reflected his

---

[1] Cf. the present writer's account in his *Foundation of Phenomenology* (2d ed.; New York: Paine-Whitman, 1962).

background in mathematics, and also his studies in the psychology of the 1880s. There is a legend to the effect that Husserl's first book was refuted by the devastating criticism of the famous mathematical philosopher, G. Frege, of Jena. It is true that Husserl had been under the influence of the psychologistic point of view ("psychologism"), according to which logic and mathematics are grounded in the psychology of thought processes. It is also true that there was some evidence of confusion in this early work, as illustrated by the unfortunate term "content." This term was widely used by psychologistic philosophers, and in Husserl's hands it led to some degree of confusion between the objective order and subjective factors. Thus it could readily be confusing to call the moon a "content." Two things may be noted, however, concerning Frege's criticism: he by no means invalidated the entire book; and he called attention to Husserl's discussion of the immediate apprehension of aggregate-characters under the heading of *"figurale Momente,"* leaving it to psychologists to evaluate its importance. It is an interesting coincidence that Husserl's emphasis upon "figural characters" should appear at about the same time as Meinong's recognition of "quasiqualitative characters" and Von Ehrenfels' discussion of *"Gestalt* qualities." This signified a correction of the narrowness of atomistic sensationalism. As Husserl expressed it, one discerns immediately the "flock character" when he observes "a flock of birds," or the "column character" when he observes "a column of soldiers." In short, "group characters" may be directly observed.

Although the *Philosophy of Arithmetic* was a youthful publication, it contained elements that were to be characteristic of the later development of Husserl's thought. Indeed, the basic problem of Husserl's later philosophy may be said to be raised at this point—the relationship between the principles of mathematics (and logic) and psychical processes. This problem was to be treated more searchingly, and in a new way, in later studies. But it is evident to the careful reader that Husserl derived his determining motivation from the attempt to unite his mathematical and psychological approaches to philosophy.

In the years that followed the publication of the *Philosophy of Arithmetic*, Husserl extended his studies in psychology and logic. This period culminated in the publication of his *Logical Investigations*, the first volume of which presented an incisive critique of "psychologism." He was well aware of the decisive nature of the step he had taken in renouncing a point of view, as well as scholars, to whom he had once felt himself close. Admitting the fact of past errors, he accounted for the severity of his criticism of the "psychologistic" logic and theory of knowledge by quoting the words of Goethe: "one is not more strict against anything than against errors only recently abandoned."

The publication of the *Logical Investigations* brought Husserl fame and academic advancement. At the University of Göttingen he had contact with mathematicians and scientists, and had the opportunity to influence students in numerous fields of scholarship. His concept of a "definite manifold," [2] for example, was presented before mathematicians and philosophers.

In 1916, Husserl received his first appointment to a full professorship of philosophy, when he was called to the University of Freiburg. There, as director of the philosophical seminar, he felt stimulated to develop his thought in the direction of a universal philosophy, which took the form of a transcendental, constitutive phenomenology. If

---

[2] Cf. E. Husserl, *Formale und transzendentale Logik* (Halle: Max Niemeyer, 1929).

his tendency may be designated idealistic, it was not to be identified with any previously existing form of idealism.

This development in the direction of idealism recalls the prediction of the neo-Kantian philosopher Paul Natorp, who was one of Husserl's early critics. In his discussion of the first volume of the *Logical Investigations*,[3] Natorp pointed out that Husserl's maintaining an "*a priori*" aligned him with the transcendental philosophy. Stating that Husserl had extended his little finger to this devil, Natorp predicted that he would have to give the whole hand. That Husserl did more than that is now evident. The reasons were to be more far-reaching and complex than Natorp could then discern.

It will be of interest to quote from Husserl's own account of his early period, which was conveyed in a letter to the present writer in 1936. He wrote:

> External "influences" are without significance. As a young beginner I naturally read much including classics and contemporary literature of the 1870s to the 1890s. I liked the critical-skeptical point of view, since I myself did not see firm ground anywhere. I was always very far removed from Kantianism and German idealism. Only Natorp interested me, more for personal reasons, and I read thoroughly the first edition of his *Introduction to Psychology*, but not the enlarged second edition. I zealously read (especially as a student) Mill's *Logic* and later the work on Hamilton's philosophy. I have repeatedly studied the English empiricists and the principal writings of Leibniz (ed. by J. E. Erdmann), especially his mathematical-philosophical writings. I first got to know Schuppe after the *Logical Investigations* when he could offer

[3] Paul Natorp, "Zur Frage der logischen Methode," *Kant-Studien*, VI (Berlin: 1901), 270–283.

me nothing further. I never looked seriously at anything by Rehmke. Really, my course was already
marked out by the *Philosophy of Arithmetic*, and I
could do nothing other than to proceed further.

This is by no means a complete list of the influences on
Husserl, however. William James interested him greatly,
particularly the *Principles of Psychology*. Husserl often
spoke of James, who helped to free him from "psychologism," and whose treatment of the "stream of consciousness" inspired Husserl in his descriptive analysis of
conscious experience. Mention should also be made of
Bolzano, Lotze, Twardowski, Marty, Avenarius, and Dilthey. Bolzano's *Wissenschaftslehre* provided him with a
first draft of a "pure logic" at a critical time in his development, and he was indebted to Lotze for his interpretation
of Plato's theory of ideas.[4] He came to know about Shadworth Hodgson after the *Logical Investigations*, when he
was pleased to credit Hodgson with insights into the subjectivistic approach to philosophy. Although it is true that
Husserl was far removed from Kant in his early period,
it is apparent that his subsequent close study of Kant made
a deep impression upon him. The influence of Kant's general program for a transcendental philosophy, and of his
theory of knowledge, is seen in Husserl's later writings,
such as his *Experience and Judgment* and his *Formal and
Transcendental Logic*. Kant was criticized for failing to
achieve a "pure" theory of knowledge, free from all naturalistic elements. In this sense, what Husserl undertook to
achieve, in his way, by means of the phenomenological
method, was what Kant had failed to do.

[4] Despite his frequently expressed appreciation of the importance of Bolzano, however, Husserl's critical judgment should
not be overlooked. Cf. M. Farber, *The Foundation of Phenomenology*, pp. 206 ff.

Finally, it may be observed that Husserl's denial of external influences is not to be regarded as plausible. Like all other thinkers, he was historically conditioned in important respects. In addition to the indebtedness to the world of philosophy already indicated (incompletely, to be sure), he was dependent upon the scientific level of his time, especially the prevailing psychology. His social attitudes were mainly the product of his German background; and his antinaturalistic tendency may also be accounted for historically, in terms of the general movement to stem the tide of philosophic naturalism and evolutionism. It is simply not true to say that "external influences are without significance." Husserl was himself far too significant a thinker (whether one agrees with him fully or largely disagrees) to allow him to be detached from the plainly evident conditions that acted upon him. Even the systematic attempt to detach the subject matter of philosophy from the natural world, which includes the cultural world, has its cultural explanation.

Husserl's early use of the term "phenomenology" was either anticipated or independently introduced at about the same time by the American philosopher, C. S. Peirce, who also used the term "phaneroscopy." The predecessors of Husserl in the great tradition of the history of philosophy are to be traced all the way back to Plato. Plato, Aristotle, medieval philosophy (especially by way of Brentano), Descartes, Leibniz, the British empiricists, and, finally, Kant, are all of them contributors to the thought of Husserl. Looking back at Descartes, Husserl stated that he was like Columbus, who discovered a new world without realizing it—the realm of pure subjectivity.

Because of so-called "racial" reasons, the last five years of Husserl's life under the Nazi rule were unhappy ones. Among his closest students, Martin Heidegger, who had become a prominent existentialist, went over to the Nazis. It is understandable that most of the "Aryan" scholars who had been indebted to him should find it disadvantageous to be associated with him. That Husserl thought much about the evils of the Third *Reich* cannot be doubted. But it was not his way to enter into the political and social movements of his time, or to take account of them. The severe restraint imposed by his philosophical views left no way of dealing with the sordid conditions that had deprived him of his human rights. He could only appeal to the judgment of eternity, with the firm confidence that he had made a lasting contribution to philosophic thought. He wrote: "And we old people remain here. A singular turn of the times: it gives the philosopher—if it does not take away his breath—much to think of. But now: *Cogito ergo sum*, i.e., I prove *sub specie aeterni* my right to live, and this, the *aeternitas* in general, cannot be touched by any earthly powers."

Although Husserl published a great deal compared with the average output of other scholars, he also had the habit of withholding much of his work, so that his published writings represented only a fraction of his complete writings. Many thousands of pages of his unpublished writings were left at his death, a large part of them in an obsolete stenographic form. It was necessary to remove the manuscripts from Germany to a place where they could be prepared for eventual publication. A visit to Freiburg by Dr. Herman Van Breda of Louvain led Mrs. Edmund Husserl to entrust that important task to him. With the recent publication of such works as the second and third volumes of Husserl's *Ideas*, his *First Philosophy*, and his *Phenomenological Psychology*, it can be expected that in a few years the most notable of his unpublished works will be available. It will then be possible for all interested persons to decide for themselves whether the real Husserl has been unknown. It is the opinion of some scholars who are acquainted with the manuscripts that they alone will truly portray the significance of Husserl. Without questioning the great importance of the manuscripts, however, it seems more reasonable to maintain that the real Husserl has indeed been rather well known in important respects from his published writings, on which he lavished so much care; and that the manuscripts will provide additional evidence of his descriptive and conceptual powers, with further helpful materials to explain the development of his ideas. There is no need to resort to extreme views. In any case, it is the image of an unfinished philosophy that emerges, not a finished system of thought.

A great number of students and scholars were indebted to Husserl, but it cannot be said that he had many close followers, at any time in his development. There were very few philosophers who accepted his views without qualification, at the time of his death; and even that small number has decreased by now. Thus, Professor Eugen Fink, who was very close to Husserl as one of his research assistants, has recently chosen to depart from the methodological position of his former master.[5] But it would be a mistake to judge the degree of influence of the phenomenological philosophy in terms of a few faithful adherents. As a matter of fact, the influence of phenomenology has been widespread and diversified.

The spirit of Husserl's work was one which forbade completion. His problems, and his ideal of a rigorous science of philosophy, had an ever open horizon. As Hus-

---

[5] Cf. E. Fink, "L'analyse intentionnelle et le problème de la pensée spéculative," in *Problèmes actuels de la Phénoménologie*, edited by H. L. Van Breda (Paris: Desclée de Brouwer, 1952).

serl first viewed phenomenology, it was the descriptive science of experience and the objects of experience, with interest restricted to their essential structures. More will have to be said about the definition of phenomenology, but this preliminary statement will help to show that it is first of all a method for philosophy, and that it is reflective and subjective in character. The phenomenological method is intended to be free from all prejudgments and dogmas. Its ideal is the elaboration of a purely descriptive philosophy by means of a well-defined, "radical" method, for which there are no initial assumptions, at least in the sense of natural experience. In its best examples, and when its own expressed intentions are strictly realized, it is a scientific tendency in philosophy. On the other hand, the nominal adoption and misuse of the phenomenological method has already illustrated the dangers of mysticism, one-sided and hence misleading description, dogmatism, and assumptive reasoning. Its competent, critical mastery, and constant awareness of the special functions and limitations of the method, should keep it free from such errors.

In the present work, most of our attention will be directed to Husserl, but some mention will be made of other members of the movement and their independent developments. Husserl's *Logical Investigations,* the most famous of his earlier works, has been widely read by students in Russia, despite the prevailing view that phenomenology, as a subjective philosophy, is in its final consequences reactionary. The same work has been extensively studied in Latin-American countries, and is in fact known to scholars everywhere. The later publications of Husserl have been read less extensively, due in part to their difficulty, but also to the more disputed direction of his development.

B. The Aims of the Phenomenological Method

The diversity of trends in the phenomenological tendency is due in part to Husserl's own development. Husserl passed through a number of different intellectual periods, and he did not succeed in convincing all the admirers of one period that they ought to go along with him in what he called "the development." Thus Karl Jaspers told him of his disappointment in what was for Husserl a decisive work in introducing transcendental phenomenology—his *Ideas* of 1913. Broadly speaking, four main periods are distinguished: (1) his early period of interest in basic problems of mathematics, as well as in a psychological approach to logic; (2) the period of the "breakthrough" to phenomenology, which was at first called "descriptive psychology" and conceived as a "neutral" field for investigation, i.e., neither idealistic nor realistic in its commitment, and in fact neutral toward all metaphysics, without "presuppositions" of any kind—in short, as a purely descriptive science; (3) the period of transcendental phenomenology, in which the reduction to the pure consciousness of an individual knower is basic; and (4) the last period of the elaboration of a constitutive idealistic philosophy which is universal in its scope, and in which some attention is given to the concepts of life and historical culture.

It was Husserl's belief that he had succeeded in giving a new foundation to philosophy. "Phenomenology" came then to be understood in two senses. There is the narrower sense of Husserl's earlier period, of phenomenology as concerned with what was formerly known as the realm of empirical psychology. Its aim is to prepare psychology as an empirical science, and to analyze and describe the various types of experience. It also investigates the "sources" out of which "arise" the fundamental concepts and ideal laws of "pure logic." These concepts and laws are to be traced back to their "sources" in conscious experience in order to procure the "clarity and distinctness" required for the epistemological understanding of logic. It should be borne in mind that the terms "sources" and "arise" are placed in quotation marks so that one does not think of any natural processes. The phenomenologist is exclusively interested in essential relations and structures, and not in particular facts or events as such, or in factual accounts of origins. In its wider sense, as developed in Husserl's later work, phenomenology is construed as "First Philosophy," and all sciences are supposed to be rooted in the domain of "pure experience" which it delineates. The "First Philosophy" which is the aim of Husserl's mature transcendental phenomenology represents his first approach to a universal system of philosophy, "valid once and for all time," which would found not only the natural and strictly formal sciences, but the "cultural" sciences as well. This requires a theory of human values and a philosophy of history. It is generally conceded that Husserl has been most successful in the fields of descriptive psychology, theory of knowledge, and logic, and less successful in the field of cultural philosophy, particularly in the treatment of history.

In the phenomenological method, one begins with an individual and his stream of experiences. This mode of beginning has its special merits, but also its limitations. If one wishes to achieve certainty in knowledge, and to examine all dogmatic and naïve beliefs, it is necessary to begin with his own conscious experiences. That is to make a "radical" beginning, and a definite field for inquiry has been marked off thereby in any case. But one may not remain restricted to his own experiences if philosophic inquiry is to have access to all regions of experience and knowledge.

Unfortunately, philosophers are subject to general human weaknesses, and one of these is to use a single method exclusively, failing to realize that a method is always adopted for the sake of a particular kind of problem. The phenomenological method is helpful for its range of problems, but it must be used in cooperation with other kinds of method. The extravagant claim that it was the only genuinely philosophical method led to a strong reaction against it, with the unfortunate result that its specific merits were forgotten or ignored.

Specifically, the phenomenological method was intended to achieve the following objectives: (1) to function as a critique of knowledge, providing clarification of basic ideas and a foundation for logic; (2) to describe essential structures of experience, as pure eidetic psychology; (3) to give as complete an account as possible of the part played by the mind in experience; (4) to provide a unified theory of science and knowledge; (5) to define explicitly the universal field for philosophical inquiry, and thus prepare the ground for descriptive analysis; this is done by defining the realm of "pure consciousness," without the usual presuppositions of the naturalistic view of the world (expressed by the ideal of freedom from presuppositions); and (6) to help realize the ideal of a complete descriptive philosophy. The phenomenological method provides a technique for the treatment of "universal" experience, i.e., all types of experience, and therewith a foundation for all knowledge. However, it must itself have a "foundation," from a different point of view. The phenomenologist undertakes to make a "radical" or an "absolute" beginning, by means of a "reduction" to pure consciousness, all things being viewed from the point of view of one's own experiencing of them, and only in so far as they have meaning in and by one's experiences. This "absolute" beginning, although an artificial construction and, as Husserl once referred to it, a "methodological device," assists us greatly in the theory of knowledge. But its place in the total enterprise of experience must not be distorted; it must never be forgotten that the phenomenologist himself is a cultural product and that even his "pure" activities are events in the natural world.

The positive aims of the phenomenological method are thus clear. The method must be reflective, "transcendental" in Kant's sense of the term, i.e., we are to attend to our experiencing of the object, rather than to the object directly; and it must be "pure" in the sense that all beliefs in natural existence (and, indeed, all judgments of existence in general) are placed in abeyance. Thus one achieves the realm of pure immanent consciousness, with its meant objects as such. It will be generally conceded that very much is to be discovered in this immanent realm; but it will not be conceded by all that *everything* is to be found there.

Negatively, the change from the "natural view" to the inspection of essences in the context of pure consciousness served the historical purpose of avoiding naturalism as a universal philosophy. An alternative to naturalism was offered. This opposition to naturalism was expressed unmistakably in Husserl's famous essay of 1911, entitled "Philosophy as a Rigorous Science." Naturalism as portrayed by Husserl is a result of the discovery of nature in the sense of a unity of spatial and temporal being, with exact laws. It sees only nature, and physical nature to begin with. All forms of consistent naturalism were opposed by Husserl as involving the "naturalizing" of consciousness and the "naturalizing" of what he called the "absolute ideals and norms." Thus he opposed not only materialism, but all other forms of naturalism, including energism, as well as positivism. He argued that naturalism suspends itself in the last analysis. He could refer to his own *Logical Investigations*, in which he had shown how untenable it was to interpret the principles of logic as laws of thought, and how this led to skepticism. Husserl thought he could similarly show how unsatisfactory was the naturalistic treatment of values. The naturalist he declared to be an idealist who sets up theories that deny what he presupposes in his idealistic attitude. The naturalist preaches, moralizes, and reforms but, in Husserl's view, he denies what is presupposed by every sermon or demand as such. With all due respect to Husserl, it must be admitted that such an argument is hardly more than an *ad hominem* charge.

It is difficult to understand how anyone could persuade himself that the naturalistic position had been undermined thereby. The ethical views of the evolutionary philosophers (Spencer, Huxley, *et al.*) certainly merited criticism. But they were not to be disposed of by means of a simple dialectical attack which not only fails to do justice to the merits of naturalistic ethics, but also provides an oversimplified version of naturalism as a convenient target. Moreover, all natural science was declared by Husserl to be naïve in its point of departure. Nature is "simply there" for it, and to know what is simply given by means of objective laws is the goal of natural science. This was applied to naturalistic psychology as well. While recognizing the ideal of scientific knowledge, Husserl was concerned with challenging the scientific philosophies of his generation. That they were vulnerable, even in terms of the existing scientific level, cannot be doubted. Husserl could say with right in his *Ideas* (Section 20): "When it is really natural science that speaks, we listen willingly and as disciples. But the language of the natural scientists is not always that of natural science itself, and is assuredly *not* so when they speak of 'natural philosophy' and the 'theory of knowledge of natural science.'" This also applies to naturalistic philosophies. Was it necessary, however, to go as far as Husserl did in his opposition to them? It is understandable that he was led to take an extremely critical position, in pointing out their defects. It is important to give a careful hearing to such criticism, so that an improved scientific philosophy may result. While by no means all Husserl's criticism of naturalistic philosophies will be accepted, it will be admitted that he has pointed out some of their defects, just as he has helped, in his positive efforts, to enlarge the field of philosophical and scientific inquiry.

II

The Ideal of Freedom
from Presuppositions

The claim of freedom from presuppositions has been made at various times, and has been held up as an ideal. In the words of Shadworth Hodgson,[1] "The philosophical problem is to find the means of philosophizing without making assumptions." The attempt to achieve a presuppositionless beginning of philosophy occurred in various ways. One was to base philosophy upon a single, ultimate principle; but it is only by a process of self-deception that the philosopher can suppose he has thereby dispensed with all assumptions. It is sufficient to recall Hegel's notion of the aseity of spirit as an example of the tradition. But Hegel's use of the dialectic method was certainly not presuppositionless. In fact, the principle of freedom from presuppositions has been called the greatest presupposition.

The principle of the aseity of spirit is at the basis of idealism. In his discussion of absolute idealism, Feuerbach pointed out that this really amounted to the restoration of a divine being to a post of honor. The materialist, of one type or another, endeavors to account for spirit either

[1] In a letter to William James, in 1882. Cf. R. B. Perry, *The Thought and Character of William James* (Boston: Little, Brown and Co., 1935), vol. I, p. 623.

18

analytically, causally, or historically. The idealist is compelled to argue for the absoluteness of spirit, which is as
little accounted for as is the impersonal God of modern
religion. This is a "substantive" assumption. It may take
the form of an absolute consciousness, a transcendental
ego, or an all-embracing mind. Leibniz accounted for his
spiritual monads by an act of divine creation; and the
divine being was provided by bad logic. The cognitive
predicament which has been used to support idealism does
not account for spirit. It is rather a way of rendering
plausible the necessity of the substantive assumption,
which is to be taken as absolute.

Empiricism also aimed at freedom from presuppositions,
using particular facts and observations as the source of
knowledge. It was effective as a weapon against authori-
tarian beliefs and rationalistic dogmas. But the strict application of the method of empiricism, which would mean
restriction to what is given in sensory experience, would be
inadequate for purposes both of science and philosophy.
That it actually does make use of assumptions is well
known. These include the recognition of principles transcending actual and even possible experience, and involving the use of conceptual devices.

Husserl chose an alternative to psychological atomism.
He adopted the descriptive method, but made it more
complete by attempting to do full justice to the essential
structure of experience and its objects; and he sought to
clarify all principles and to "constitute" all things on the
basis of "pure consciousness," a realm purged of all beliefs
in transcendent existence. There were to be no "presuppositions," at least in the ordinary sense of the term. Radicalism of method was the aim of Husserl's phenomenological
investigations from their beginning. His original studies in
the theory of knowledge were made to conform to the
ideal of freedom from presuppositions, which was derived

from the earlier philosophical writings of the 1880s, his immediate philosophical background. It is proposed in this chapter to consider the meaning of this ideal, which requires first the distinction of the various meanings of "presupposition"; then the meaning such an ideal may have for logic and the theory of knowledge; and finally the question of the foundation of phenomenology itself.

A. The Meaning of "Presupposition"

The term "presupposition" is highly ambiguous. Literally it means "posited as holding or as existing in advance." Because of its many uses the term must be interpreted in a twofold manner, as referring to existence as well as to thought. In its broadest meaning it refers to any kind of supposition or assumption,[2] such as a material or ideal domain, a realm of existence, a process of experience, or a system of knowledge. It may also be taken to refer to formal principles, either in the sense of arbitrary assumptions or of necessary logical principles.

The following classification of types of presupposition will be helpful. (a) There are material presuppositions, which are either physical in their reference, or relate to domains of abstract things. In the world of experience, for example, the continuity of existence in time, the independence of existence with regard to cognition, causal uniformity, and infinite extension in *macro* as well as in *micro* terms, are generally considered to be basic presuppositions. (b) Mention is often made of cognitive presuppositions, such as the reliability of perception and memory, and the validity of knowledge. These should not be treated as assumptions, however, but as results to be achieved. Our

[2] Cf. Husserl, *Ideas*, p. 455.

ability to know reality truly does not have to be assumed if all known evidence overwhelmingly verifies it. (c) There are formal assumptions in special systems. The postulational method is a practical matter, and is employed because of human limitations and purposes. In the nature of the case the systems of knowledge could not be dealt with actually as simple wholes. The distinction between assumptions and deductions is a response to the problem of the statement of knowledge, which admits of alternatives, and of the deductive demonstration of propositions. No one set of propositions could be singled out as the necessary foundation of a system. This is different from (d) the principles of logic, which are peculiarly fundamental and which do not admit of alternatives, although they may be defined in different ways. Thus they may be taken to apply to the infinite system of all conceivable propositions, or only to those which can be verified or constructed. For a completely formal or "realistic" logic, they apply to the entire structure of knowledge and are requirements imposed upon any systems or parts of knowledge. The question just which principles are to serve as postulates of logic is not different from the case of the special systems mentioned in (c), for the system of logic has the properties of a special system. It merely happens that its structure as a system is determined by its own laws. There are equivalent alternative postulate sets for logic; but these are to be distinguished from alternative versions of logical principles—such as the principle of the excluded middle, for example—in their range of application, as is illustrated by intuitionism and formalism. The cherished "gilt-edged" principles of the traditional logic, the "laws of thought," may appear as theorems in the system of logic; but they are no more necessary than any other logical principles. This is not to imply, however, that all sets of logical propositions are on the same level so far as deductive power is

concerned. In this sense, "logically prior" may be taken to
mean "deductively more powerful." [3]

Other possible meanings of the term "presupposition"
should be mentioned for completeness. These include motivation, influences, significance for society and history, as
well as beliefs. According to Brentano,[4] for example, the
term "presuppositionless" meant "free from prejudice" or
from prejudgments. The requirement that the cultural sciences should proceed without presuppositions was understood to mean freedom from world-view assumptions.[5]
Motives, as one kind of presupposition, were eliminated by
Husserl in his use of the phenomenological method;[6] or
rather, only phenomenological motives were allowed.
There were to be no motives derived from the natural
world, or from any non-phenomenological realm, any more
than there were to be prejudgments. The attempt to dispense with presuppositions in all meanings of the term
requires the disregard, or the suspension, of all traditional
formal and non-formal assumptions. It must lead to a mind
divested not only of all bodiliness, but also of all real and
ideal conditions of experience and thought. It would seem

[3] Cf. C. I. Lewis' discussion of presuppositions in *Mind and
the World-Order* (New York: Charles Scribner's Sons, 1929),
pp. 200 ff., 415 ff.

[4] In his anonymous article, "Über voraussetzungslose Forschung" (1901), which deals with freedom of thought and investigation. Cf. F. Brentano, *Die vier Phasen der Philosophie und
ihr augenblicklicher Stand* (Leipzig: Meiner, 1926), pp. 137–
144.

[5] Cf. E. Spranger, "Der Sinn der Voraussetzungslosigkeit in
den Geisteswissenschaften," *Sitzungsberichte der Preussischen
Akademie der Wissenschaften* (Berlin, 1929), pp. 2–30.

[6] Cf. E. Fink, "Die phänomenologische Philosophie Edmund
Husserls in der gegenwärtigen Kritik," *Kant-Studien* (Berlin,
1933).

that solipsism is the unavoidable beginning. If one's quest for ultimate understanding leads him to such a basis, he must be prepared to pass beyond solipsism. The phenomenological method undertakes to meet this problem.

B. The Conception of a Presuppositionless Theory of Knowledge

The need for the clarification of logic by the theory of knowledge was urged by Husserl at the beginning of the century, and it was a task which led him to examine the fundamental ideas of the theory of knowledge as well as to set up the ideal of a philosophical beginning without presuppositions. As he expressed it later, this meant that pure logic was to be "bracketed" along with everything else. The method of reflective analysis, as developed by him, was intended to make possible a final foundation of logic and philosophy.

The requirement that the theory of knowledge be free from presuppositions was prominent in the literature of Husserl's older contemporaries. In his essay on the theory of knowledge as a presuppositionless science, Volkelt [7] pointed out that all sciences except epistemology presuppose the possibility of knowledge. In his view, epistemology must precede all other sciences, and may not make logical, psychological, or metaphysical assumptions. In

[7] In 1881 Volkelt expressed the ideal of freedom from presuppositions in "Die Aufgabe und die Fundamentalschwierigkeit der Erkenntnistheorie als einer voraussetzungslosen Wissenschaft," a paper published in the *Philosophische Monatschefte*, XVII (Berlin, 1881), 513–541. Cf. also Volkelt's *Erfahrung und Denken* (Hamburg and Leipzig: Vosa, 1886); *Gewissheit und Wahrheit* (München: Beck, 1918).

order to make an indubitable beginning and to avoid circularity, he began with his own consciousness. Since he restricted himself to that which is absolutely self-evident, there could be no talk of other minds, or of general propositions which are ordinarily assumed as principles. Volkelt's indubitable sphere of consciousness proved to be devoid of promise, for he declared that nothing of regularity or law or connection could be discovered in it. He was unable to give a satisfactory answer to the question how the epistemologist is to get out of the sphere of his own consciousness. His program for epistemology was intended to make clear the extent of knowing and the degrees of certainty.

As expressed in his *Certainty and Truth*, Volkelt's requirement of freedom from presuppositions means that the theory of knowledge must begin with a self-evident proposition to which immediate certainty is attached without restriction. Even logic may not form the basis of epistemology. Propositions derived from logic or psychology must be gained by means of epistemology. They must either be certain in themselves, or possess certainty by virtue of being inferences from other already-established propositions, which ultimately are known to be self-evident. Thus knowledge belonging to other sciences can be brought within the framework of epistemology. Volkelt's proposal to dispense with the assumption of the independent validity of mathematics and science clearly shows his conception of the radical ideal of critically examining all knowledge and belief. The truth of science is presupposed in the investigation of the "transcendental" basis of scientific knowledge, and hence such a theory of knowledge cannot be fundamental. The "transcendental presupposition" was made by Kant, Windelband, and others. As distinguished from them, Volkelt attempted to make epistemology presuppositionless, in accordance with its definition as the science of the validity of knowledge, or of the

possibility of knowledge. As he stated it, to assume the
validity of knowledge for being would reduce the entire
undertaking to a comedy. Volkelt's "epistemological
epoché" corresponds to Husserl's phenomenological suspension of judgment and belief, but his belief that he had
fulfilled by epistemology what Husserl requires for phenomenology can only be justified if one mistakes the will
for the deed. Recognition of the general programmatic
nature of a presuppositionless theory of knowledge designed to serve as a "First Philosophy" is not equivalent to
the rigorous formulation of the necessary method. Volkelt's
type of analysis failed to offer even a remote equivalent of
the elaborate and painstaking descriptive analyses which
make up the real content of phenomenology.

It will be sufficient, finally, to mention Schuppe's and
Rehmke's views as illustrations of the prephenomenologi-
cal treatment of the problem. Schuppe [8] agreed with Volkelt in regarding epistemology as the fundamental science.
He interpreted "freedom from presuppositions" as meaning
that only those presuppositions are made without which
the undertaking itself would be devoid of meaning and
content. These include a conscious being, the doubt of the
epistemologist, a concept of truth and error, and the required activity of thought. Schuppe had also tried to follow
the line of Descartes' method of doubt, but was no more
successful than Volkelt in finding a way which led to something outside of the thinking consciousness. He merely
posed the problem.

By the freedom from presuppositions of a science,
Rehmke [9] understood the requirement that no determina-

[8] W. Schuppe, "Zur 'voraussetzungslosen' Erkenntnistheorie,"
Philosophische Monatshefte, XVIII (Berlin, 1882), 375–386.

[9] Johannes Rehmke, *Philosophie als Grundwissenschaft*
(Frankfurt: Kesselring, 1910), pp. 40 ff. Cf. also his *Anmer-
kungen zur Grundwissenschaft* (Leipzig: Barth, 1913).

tions concerning its particular subject-matter are to be accepted in advance of its investigation; that would be to make prejudgments. Only the fundamental science of philosophy is completely free from prejudgments. Historical science, for example, assumes "consciousness simply" or "man simply" as determinately given. Rehmke emphasized the difference between freedom from presuppositions and from prejudgments: for science, only the second concept applies, since a presuppositionless science would be impossible; this holds also for the fundamental science, which presupposes "givenness simply" and nothing further. And, apart from that, it places everything in question.

A survey of the relevant literature shows that there is a vast difference between the general aim of achieving for a philosophy the status of a fundamental science, and the actual elaboration of a method to realize it. The time was in fact ripe to provide the latter.

C. Formal Reasoning and the Reflexive Predicament

The problem of the "founding" of logic was of central importance to Husserl, and provided the initial motivation for the development of a universal phenomenological method. It will therefore be well to consider first the question of the self-sufficiency of formal reasoning.

Usually there are characteristic concepts and postulates that distinguish a special system of knowledge. The ideal of deduction is to construct all knowledge homogeneously, which means in terms of one basis. Basic conceptual unity has been achieved in principle in formal science; the fundamental concepts of logic have been shown to be adequate for the construction of mathematical concepts. The former, however, stand in need of further investigation.

The attempt to determine the fundamental principles of logic involves the question of the circularity of formal reasoning. Formal reasoning is circular for the same reason that all terms cannot be defined; i.e., universal demonstration is as impossible as universal definition, *as a matter of presentation*. It is impossible to prove all propositions, for there must always be an assumed basis for demonstration. This restriction refers exclusively to the medium of reasoning and not to the particular nature of the propositions. It cannot be said that any particular significant proposition is incapable of proof, even though it is true that all propositions are not thus capable of proof, at least within deduction. In a well-founded system, significant propositions, or propositions which are proper to the given system, are essentially either true or false. There is no inherent reason why they may not be proved to be one or the other. The question of our finite, human ability to prove or disprove propositions does not enter into the problem of circularity; rather, it concerns the foundation of the principles of logic. Assumptions must be made in all reasoning, including reasoning in logic itself. The attempt to demonstrate any of the principles of logic requires the use of premises, and either a part of logic is involved therewith, or another and perhaps larger system of propositions. The essence of the method of deduction is really in question here.

The aim of formal reasoning is to operate as far as possible with purely formal structures. The sharp delimitation of formal logic is necessary for the development of the science. All philosophical or non-formal considerations must therefore be eliminated. Husserl's judgment that the traditional logic is grounded in the world of mundane existence does not hold for symbolic logic, which is kept as free from all non-formal elements as possible. But it does presuppose a possible world for its realization. The importance and significance of epistemological, psychological, and ontological questions pertaining to logic cannot be denied, for logic is admittedly not a self-sufficient discipline. Deductive reasoning involves cognitive operations, if not actually, then possibly, "as though" such processes were carried out. This applies not only to such operations as substitution and inference, but also to the process of idealization, which provides the ideal objects and relations of logic. It is becoming increasingly clear that logic requires the preparatory analysis of meaning and the concept of reality. The reference to something objective presents a problem for which the analysis of meaning and symbolism is necessary. The fundamental principles of knowledge which govern truth and meaning apply to all systems. The crucial question for a presuppositionless philosophy, as far as deduction is concerned, is whether it is possible to examine the grounds and processes of knowledge in such a way that the fundamental concepts and principles are evident, as a prelogical undertaking. In short, there are presuppositions of logic which concern its cognitive aspects, endow it with the element and criteria of meaning (thus constituting its subject-matter), and provide for its reference to an objective realm.

The self-foundation of formal logic must be supplemented by another dimension of investigation. The phenomenological treatment of logic has the function of clarifying its basic ideas, and also of providing its very elements by means of the descriptive analysis of such concepts as "judgment" and "meaning." The concepts of the understanding, and hence all of the ideas used on the higher level of formal reasoning, are traced to their "origin" in pre-predicative experience.[10] This procedure is designated "genetic," not in an empirical, factual, or historical

[10] In the language of Husserl's *Erfahrung und Urteil,* edited by L. Landgrebe (Prague: Academia Verlag, 1939).

sense, but in the sense of the intentional reference of all ideas or principles to their "original" evidences—in the last analysis, to the direct evidence of individuals. The element of historical time is simply irrelevant to such analysis. Husserl regarded the domain of the logical as much greater than in the traditional logic. Logical "contribution" was found by him to be present on all levels of experience, not only on the comparatively high level on which the traditional logic begins in its analysis. But he held that it is on the lower levels that the concealed presuppositions are to be found, on the basis of which the evidences of the logician on a higher level are to be understood.

The logocentric predicament is incurred, as Sheffer has pointed out,[11] because of the need to presuppose and employ logic in order to give an account of logic. This difficulty is met by attempting to make explicit that which is assumed to be valid, and by the use of a kind of formal *epoché*, which makes it possible to distinguish sharply between the study of formal structure and its interpretation in terms of any kind of objectivity, and also between both of these and the study of the conditions that make considerations of notation and interpretation significant and valid. Even if the logocentric predicament could be avoided by means of a purely intuitive method, another predicament would take its place on the epistemological level. In order to investigate cognition, it is necessary to make use of knowledge. This is sufficiently justified in the course of the investigation, but it must nevertheless be regarded as an assumption for the initial purpose of epistemological analysis, one that is unavoidable because of the essentially reflexive character of philosophic inquiry. Corresponding to the formal *epoché* (in which abstraction is made from all concrete, sensory meanings) but more

[11] Cf. *Isis*, VIII (Brussels, 1926), 226 ff.

sweeping in its extent, is the epistemological *epoché,* which
suspends all logical, psychological, and ontological principles. This is necessary for the thoroughgoing descriptive
analysis of cognition. The degree of clarification is thereby
greatly increased, for lower levels of cognition may be investigated by means of "genetic" analyses. As in the case
of the logocentric predicament, there is no insurmountable
difficulty, provided that all tentatively assumed elements
are made explicit.

D. The Program of Phenomenology

The ideal of freedom from presuppositions as applied to
logic and the theory of knowledge was recognized in the
Logical Investigations,[12] and as applied to philosophy as
a whole in the *Logos* essay, "Philosophy as a Rigorous
Science." The mechanism for this ideal was first provided
by the method of phenomenological reduction, which was
systematically presented in the *Ideas* and *Cartesian Meditations.*

The phenomenological studies in the *Logical Investigations* were preparatory in character. From Husserl's
statement that a scientific investigation in the theory of
knowledge must satisfy the requirement of freedom from
presuppositions, it can be inferred that this ideal was recognized by him as the acid test of a truly critical philosophy. In his view, this meant the strict exclusion of all
assertions which could not be completely realized phenomenologically—i.e., in terms of intuitive experience alone
—and subject to well-defined conditions. The "theory" to
be achieved is simply the reflective and evident under-

[12] *Logische Untersuchungen* (Halle: Max Niemeyer, 1901),
vol. II, pp. 19 ff.

standing of the nature of thinking and knowing in general. Acts of thought may refer to transcendent or even to non-existent and impossible objects. But the meaning of such experiences is clarified purely on the basis of the experience. The justification of the assumption of "physical" and "psychical" realities that transcend consciousness is not proper to the pure theory of knowledge; the question of the existence and nature of the "external world" is metaphysical. It is true that epistemology, as the general explanation of the ideal essence and valid meaning of thought, considers the question of the possibility of knowing "real" objects or things, which are essentially transcendent to the experiences by which they are known, and the nature of the norms of such knowledge. But it is not concerned with the empirical question, whether human beings can actually gain such knowledge on the basis of the factual data given to them.

As Husserl regarded it, epistemology is really not a theory at all; it is not a science in the pregnant sense of a unity of theoretical explanation. Its aim is not the construction of deductive theories. This is shown by the most general theory of knowledge which Husserl described in the *Prolegomena*[13] as the philosophical supplement to the pure mathesis, which comprises all *a priori* categorial knowledge in the form of systematic theories. The "formal" theory of knowledge, which explains this theory of theories, is prior to all empirical theory; hence it is prior to all explanatory real science, to physical science and psychology, and also to metaphysics. It aims, not to explain the factual occurrence of knowledge in objective nature in a psychological or psychophysical sense, but rather to clarify the idea of knowledge with respect to its consti-

[13] *Logische Untersuchungen* (Halle: Max Niemeyer, 1901), vol. I.

tutive elements and laws. It is interested in understanding the ideal meaning of the connections of experience, in which the objectivity of knowledge is documented, and seeks to bring the pure forms and laws of knowledge to clarity and distinctness by recourse to adequately fulfilled intuition. This clarification occurs within the framework of a phenomenology of knowledge which is concerned with the essential structures of the "pure" experiences and their meanings. There is no assertion concerning real existence, and hence no use can be made of premises drawn from metaphysics or natural science, especially psychology. It is this metaphysical, natural-scientific, and psychological freedom from presuppositions, *and no other kind,* that Husserl proposed to realize at this time. If reference was made to actual languages and the merely communicative meaning of some of their forms of expression, he did not overstep the limits of his inquiry, for the analyses presented would retain their meaning and epistemological value regardless of whether there are actually languages and intercourse between people, or whether there are people and a world of nature. The analyses would hold even if everything existed only in the imagination, or as a possibility. The only premises recognized by Husserl are those that meet the requirement of adequate phenomenological justification, which means fulfillment through evidence in the strictest sense of the term.

The conception of philosophy advanced in his *Logos* essay, in which philosophy is portrayed as a discipline that provides the sciences with a new dimension and a final completion, indicates the universal scope of Husserl's analysis. He emphasized the importance of the radical criticism of the naturalistic philosophy, urging a positive critique of its foundations and methods. The term "radical" is a popular one in phenomenology. Negatively it spells

freedom from assumptions or beliefs of any kind, and positively it signifies the insightful establishment of all elements
of knowledge. In Husserl's view, the natural sciences are
"naïve" with respect to their points of departure.[14] For
them, nature is "simply there," and things *are* in infinite
space and time; they are "pregiven." The same holds for
things from the standpoint of psychology. Every psychological judgment posits physical nature as existent, whether
explicitly or not. It follows that if physical natural science
cannot be philosophy, then neither can psychology, which
is based upon it. The "naïveté" with which nature is regarded as given for natural science is "immortal" in it, as
Husserl expressed it. He recognized the fact that natural
science is very critical in its way, which is satisfactory as
long as we remain in natural science and think with its
attitude. But, he contended, a different critique of experience is both possible and necessary, a critique which places
all experience in question and, along with it, experiential-
scientific thinking. The proposed critique requires that all
scientific and prescientific asssertions concerning nature, or
all statements which imply that things are posited as existent in space, time, causal connection, etc., must be eliminated on principle. This procedure was extended to include
the elimination of the existence of the investigator himself,
or his psychical faculties and the like.

The clarification of consciousness and of all forms of
objectivity is undertaken by phenomenology, and its procedure is supposed to be radical in the sense that no existence is assumed. This is made possible by essential
intuition, in which an essence is grasped without positing
any existence. Essences can be "seen" just as immediately
as tones can be heard; for example, the essence "tone,"

[14] *Logos,* I (Tübingen, 1911), p. 298.

or the essences "thing-appearance," "visible thing," "judg-ment," etc. Pure phenomenology was defined by Husserl (in the *Logos* essay) as a science that investigates essences alone, and not as concerned with the investigation of exist-ence, or with "self-observation." The knowledge of essences and of essential relations was held to provide all that is necessary for the clarification of empirical knowledge and of all knowledge. Such knowledge was regarded as being prior to empirical knowledge, in the sense that the essen-tial knowledge of the psychical is presupposed by all psychological knowledge.

If the procedure is to be thoroughly radical, no "pregiven-ness" may be allowed; nothing is to be handed down for a beginning.[15] Inasmuch as philosophy is defined as being essentially the science of true beginnings or origins, the science of the radical must be required to be radical in its procedure in every respect. The method of philosophy is, in short, a method of direct intuition. The phenomenologi-cal grasping of essences opens up an endless field for work, providing knowledge without any indirect symbolism and mathematical methods, without the apparatus of inference and proof. This appears to be the most rigorous type of knowledge.

Husserl's motives were thus given a vigorous expression, and this early account has the advantage of formulating clearly the general program which his later work has ex-tended and deepened. The *Ideas* presented a much more detailed account of this program, and introduced the method and technique of phenomenological reduction. Characteristic of the work is the orientation to Descartes, in particular the method of doubt. In Descartes' hands the method was nugatory. As employed in phenomenology, it is of aid in determining the ultimate grounds of knowl-

[15] *Op. cit.*, p. 340.

edge, and also in providing a universal plane of experience and knowledge.

The phenomenological method is not only a possible method for the theory of knowledge, but one which necessarily must be developed and carried through consciously for the understanding of the nature and structure of knowledge. In fact, it has been tacitly assumed and used in part in the past. It is to Husserl's credit that he was able to elaborate it systematically as a descriptive method applied to pure experience, i.e., independent of the thesis or belief in spatio-temporal "natural existence," but including that realm in its scope. It would be a misunderstanding of the method to expect it to derive existence by means of a device that abstracts from existence. The positive program of phenomenology is devoted to the task of the "constitution" of the world of nature and culture. Interpreted properly as a method of construction, in accordance with the descriptive ideal of phenomenology, the procedure is a legitimate part of the theory of science or of knowledge. Husserl spoke[16] of the "constitution of objectivity as referred to its subjective source" as one phase of his inquiry. This indicates the importance of determining the scope of constitutive phenomenology. Does it comprise reality, or possible reality, throughout; or is it concerned merely with the constitution of objectivity in this relationship to subjectivity, which is of course a possible and defensible theme? The second alone is meaningful for phenomenology. One must be careful not to interpret constitution as a creative activity in a metaphysical sense, if the method is to be kept free from dogma. This is not to suggest that there is no creative element in experience; the examination of the creative performances of the understanding, for

---

[16] *Ideas,* p. 234.

example, is also a matter for accurate descriptive analysis.[17]

E. Is Anything Assumed in Phenomenology?

The question whether anything is assumed in phenomenology must now be considered. Take, for example, Husserl's statement,[18] that "the stream of experience cannot begin and end." The same could be said of consciousness, in his view. The consciousness or experience of individual beings begins and ends. Which consciousness or stream of experience may be meant? It can only be an absolute process, the phenomenological status of which must then be established. And what shall be said of the permanent, objective validity of essential insight, or of the uniformity of the constitutive process itself, the fixed, temporal structure of consciousness, the validity of memory, and the egos of various types of construction? These must be justified by phenomenological analysis.

The bulk of Husserl's discussions of method shows that he does not acknowledge the use of assumed elements and constructions. They have no place in a philosophy conceived as a rigorous science with a final foundation.[19] No alleged self-evident elements may function as an unquestioned ground of knowledge in a science which is charged with final self-responsibility. Of course, something may not be unquestioned, and may nevertheless be as-

[17] Cf. *Erfahrung und Urteil*, Part II.
[18] *Ideas*, p. 236.
[19] Cf. Husserl, "Nachwort zu meinen Ideen zu einer reinen Phänomenologie," *Jahrbuch für Philosophie und phänomenologische Forschung*, XI (Halle, 1930), 549–570. This is Husserl's introduction to the English edition of the *Ideas*, plus a preface of about three pages, to which reference is made here.

sumed, at least provisionally. Husserl's ideal of philosophy
was held to be realizable in an infinite historical process.
The radical reflection which is required examines systematically "the ultimate thinkable presuppositions" of knowledge. The reflective inquiry leads first to the "universal
subjective being and life" which is presupposed as prescientific in all theorizing, and then proceeds to the "transcendental subjectivity," which is regarded as the primal source
of all endowment of meaning and verification of being.
Husserl called attention to the new meaning of the expression "transcendental subjectivity," the retention of which
was an unhappy circumstance. This rigorous science of
philosophy was held to be a universal and absolutely founding discipline, and there was no doubt about its being advanced as something essentially new. Husserl warned
against transcendental anthropologism and psychologism
as dangers besetting those who fail to reach the real ground
of philosophy by means of the phenomenological reduction. If the procedure is thoroughgoing, no elements of an
empirical or *a priori* anthropology are retained.

In the continuation of his description of the phenomenological method,[20] Husserl distinguished between ordinary presuppositions of a positive kind and what is
presupposed implicitly in all presupposing and in all questioning and answering. The latter was held to exist necessarily, and to continue to exist, and was not acknowledged
to be an assumption. It was regarded rather as the first
thing to be freely and expressly posited, and that "with a
self-evidence which precedes all conceivable instances of
self-evidence, and is contained implicitly in them all."

That his repeated declarations on the presuppositionless
ideal of philosophy did not refer to assumptions in every
sense of the term is thus shown by Husserl's last published

[20] Cf. the author's preface to the English edition of the *Ideas*.

writings. The absolute basis which philosophy secures for itself was declared by Husserl to constitute the totality of presuppositions that can be taken for granted.[21] This was stated more pointedly in an article on phenomenology,[22] in which he wrote that the transcendental problem derives the means of its solution from an existence-stratum which it presupposes and sets beyond the reach of its inquiry. This realm was described as the bare subjectivity of consciousness in general. All knowledge was to be founded upon this basis by referring everything to the "transcendental origin." Husserl's idealistic position was clearly indicated by his thesis that all objective existence is essentially "relative," owing its nature to a unity of intention which is established according to transcendental laws.

F. Significance of the Ideal

The problem of presuppositions owes its prominence to the idealistic argument on the priority of thought over being. It derives from the cognitive approach to philosophy, beginning with the individual knower and his object, which has its historical explanation. That is one line of development leading to transcendental idealism, with its *a priori* construction of thought forms, and to transcendental phenomenology, designed to be the self-clarifying, constitutive basis of all knowledge. Another line of development proceeds from the "logic of the world" to abstractions or logical forms and their deductive arrangement, giving rise to the question of the circularity of logic and the status

---

[21] *Ideas*, p. 28. Cf. also E. Fink, "Das Problem der Phänomenologie Edmund Husserls," *Revue internationale de Philosophie*, I (1939).

[22] *Encyclopaedia Britannica*, 14th ed., XVII (1927), 701 ff.

of its fundamental principles. These were conceived by Husserl to hold unconditionally, in accordance with the "logical absolutism" of the *Logical Investigations,* a position given a transcendental foundation by his later logical studies. We are thus referred to the self-foundation of phenomenology as a theory of knowledge.

It has been seen that what Husserl calls the "genetic method" differs from what is ordinarily understood as the naturalistic genetic method. The latter operates within the space–time framework of the actual world; for it, things have a history, and the temporal order is essential. Thus the mental development of a particular individual is traced back to the earliest formation of abstractions, or there is interest in the development from the first blurred confusion of experience to distinct ideas and the discrimination of the elements of experience. For the phenomenological genetic method, all actual, historical individuals are of no interest as such; abstraction is made from the real temporal order. An idealized meaning, for example, is traced back essentially to the simpler experience it presupposes; ultimately this means the experience of individuals. This is similar to the way in which remembrance as such refers back to an original perception.

This method is presuppositionless in a way that formal logic is not and cannot be, for formal logic operates on the "higher" level of idealizations. If everything is to be placed in question and understood by recourse to primitive experience, the idealizations of logic must be accounted for. The phenomenological method, with its technique of reduction and essential analysis, may be the most radical of all methods, if used correctly. The intentional analysis of the cognitive process, when restricted to cognition and its correlates as such, may well be the most critical possible beginning for philosophy.

In logic, one operates with proposition-meanings and

structures that represent past products of intellectual activity. There are two possible ways of retracing their "origin": first, to go back to their actual historical origination in the minds of particular thinkers; and second, to proceed from the actual matters of fact merely in order to "remake" or "constitute" them, by going back to their perceptual, judgmental basis and showing how they arise essentially. It is this second procedure which is adopted by phenomenology. The exclusive consideration of essential structures and relations is the first step; and the phenomenological reduction makes possible the final elucidation of all elements of knowledge and experience by enabling us to get back of and to the bottom of all presuppositions. Because this means the reduction to the conscious life of an individual knower to begin with, as the basis for all later constitutive activity, and because the perception of individuals is the starting point, this method contributes to the realization of a radical philosophy.

What is assumed at this point? Not the spatio-temporal world; none of the scientific theories which are used to interpret the world of existence; no independent or continuous existence; no other human beings; not one's own bodily existence or empirically conditioned ego; not the ideal science of pure logic, nor any of the idealizations of theoretical knowledge: in short, nothing is assumed; as a beginning there is only the self-validating cognitive experience itself. The "world" is, to be sure, "pregiven." But that region of pregivenness whose acknowledgment rules out the one-sidedness of subjective idealism plays no role in the constitutive method itself. It is used as a guiding thread, or as a clue, just as the traditional logic is used. They are provisional presuppositions. When constituted "originally," they are no longer presuppositions. As far as the individual knower is concerned, the constitutive process represents an infinite task.

In his *Experience and Judgment*, Husserl stated that the being of the world is not achieved through a judgmental activity, but is the presupposition of all judging. If one apprehends an object, he discerns it as having been there previously, even if he were not attending to it. Thus all existence that affects us does so on the ground of the world; it is given to us as supposed existence, and the activity of knowledge aims to test whether it is truly such as it is supposed. The world as an existent world was regarded by Husserl as the universal passive pregivenness of all judgmental activity, of all theoretical interest that might enter in. As Husserl maintained, however, the concept of a presupposition receives a new meaning in the radicalism of transcendental phenomenology. The "world," which was the basis of all previous philosophies, is always present as a domain that is already valid, just as it is in everyday life. But it is not an explicit premise. In phenomenology, an *epoché* is performed upon this fixed, posited being. The "pregiven world" is finally regarded as constituted by transcendental subjectivity. To attain to this, one must proceed from the "original life-world" to the subjective "contributions" from which the life-world arises. In this sense, transcendental logic investigates the role of the logical contributions of consciousness in the construction of the world.

The examination of all assumptions, including its own, is made possible by the phenomenological method, which in its complete form includes reference to historical and cultural meanings; to these may be added the inspection of the method itself with regard to its place in history and culture. There need be no narrowness; nothing need be inaccessible to a truly descriptive method. The method of intentional analysis has the additional advantage of extending the field for description. The thoroughgoing justification of this method is not accomplished at one stroke, but must be achieved progressively. That is the task of the critical self-justification of all knowledge upon the basis of the self-givenness of the objects of experience.

The ideal of freedom from presuppositions—illustrated by Husserl's actual procedure in his investigations, including his logical as well as epistemological writings in all periods of his development—requires that there be no unexamined assumptions of any kind; that there be no metaphysical or existential assumptions unless there is a special reason for explicitly positing them; and that there be no prejudgments. It properly means the explicit examination and constitutive analysis of all elements of the structure of knowledge and reality. In contributing toward that end, Husserl has made one of the most striking advances in recent philosophy.

III

Phenomenology as a Method

A. The Descriptive Program

The early formulation of phenomenology as descriptive psychology and theory of knowledge was soon found to be inadequate. The term "phenomenology" meant the descriptive analysis of thought-experiences "to a greater extent than had occurred before," as Husserl stated it in reply to a critic. As Husserl argued, it would be nonsense to think of ordering the realm of pure logic, or of formal science, under psychology. The "critique of knowledge" provided by phenomenology includes an investigation of the "origin" of the concepts and laws of pure logic. The critical elucidation of pure logic goes beyond logic, and involves a study of the subjective acts of meaning and their relationship to objective structures. Such a study could not be expected of psychology; not, that is to say, of psychology as an empirical science of mental facts, operating within the framework of a natural science. For the more thorough-going understanding of experience, the natural world and all metaphysical beliefs are suspended, or are placed in abeyance. Since the descriptions of phenomenology do not refer to the experiences of actual empirical persons, it would be wrong to designate phenomenology as descriptive psychology in the usual sense. Nothing is said about human beings, and no hypotheses are made. A phenomenological description deals with what is given in experience as such, with experiences just as they are in themselves. The aim is to bring to evident consciousness the essence of that which is experienced. It is possible to return to the psychological point of view at any time, and to restore the assumptions which were suspended. Thus the results of phenomenology may be applied and made useful. The phenomenological analyses then function as descriptive psychological analyses, and they serve as bases for the theoretical explanations of psychology as a natural science. Because Husserl was regarded as being hostile to psychology, but also because of the special vocabulary and difficulty of his writings, there has been far too little recognition of the possible fruitfulness of his findings for psychology. He denied hostility toward psychology, but at times seemed to go further than was required by the criticism of psychologism and naturalism.

In an important systematic sense, phenomenology may be regarded as the "first science," although not in every sense. Metaphysics could not be considered the "first science," because it follows the special sciences and is dependent upon them. If all aspects of experience are to be examined and understood, metaphysics must be suspended, along with all other judgments. The very concept of being is clarified in phenomenology, so that phenomenology is held to be prior in this sense to metaphysics, as well as to all other disciplines. This may well be true from the point of view of a knower who challenges all beliefs concerning matters of fact, or existence as a whole, for the sake of reexamining them in terms of immediate evidence. But in another sense (in terms of the established matters of fact) the phenomenologist himself is a latecomer in the evolutionary process, and he must himself "follow" everything, including a naturalistic metaphysics. This would not be granted by Husserl, of course. In his early "neutral" period, Husserl was careful to avoid the pitfalls of philosophical idealism, as well as what he held to be the philosophically "naïve" view of an independent order of natural existence. When he finally took the line of idealism himself, he really abandoned the strict use of the phenomenological method to that extent.

A purely descriptive method is admittedly an ideal, and numerous difficulties stand in the way of its attainment. There may be errors due to dogmatic or unconsciously accepted interpretations in the case of phenomenological reflection, just as there are errors in ordinary external perception. But description does not lose its value because of the occurrence of errors. Husserl's famous slogan, "Back to the things themselves!", emphasizes the aim of dealing only with what is given in direct experience. Consequently, there is no room for "speculative constructions" in phenomenology. The phenomenological *epoché*, or suspension of beliefs, forbids such constructions. With its interest in description in all regions of experience, phenomenology appears as a new science, within the well-defined limits of pure experience. In keeping with its program of attending only to essential relations and structures, all its findings are matters of essential insight.

It is the aim of description to give an account of all the pertinent facts; it cannot be an account of *all* the facts, because the facts are infinite in number. This may be illustrated in the field of history. If one considers the view that it is the function of the historian to give an account of the past as it actually occurred, then he encounters fundamental difficulties at once. There is the historian's own viewpoint to be considered; he has his beliefs, conscious or unconscious, his cultural conditioning, his class and personal bias. It would be presuming a good deal to claim that a given historian has rendered "the past as it actually occurred," even if he succeeded in recovering a great many of the facts. Analogous to the difficulties in the way of experience and knowledge, which have been a favorite theme of the skeptics, there are not only the difficulties resulting from the individual or the group which conditions him, but also the problems caused by the facts themselves; and there is the necessity of weighing the evidence of events which continue to recede into the past. If the average person, and possibly all persons, may be said to be limited by "blinkers" (Husserl's term was "*Scheuklappen*," the name for the blinkers placed at both sides of a horse's head to prevent fright) he may also be said to wear "spectacles," and to see the world as an already interpreted phenomenon. The "spectacles" are the result of past scientific inquiry and fixed traditional conceptions. It is an aim of phenomenological description to get back of all such "spectacles," and to view the "blinkers" in their role in experience, so that a completely "original" description is possible. This is an ideal, of course. It turns out that phenomenological description is most successful in the field of logical experience, for example in its "origin-analyses" of logical forms such as relation, modality, etc. Husserl did not apply this method, or any other phase of the phenomenological procedure, to actual cultural conditions. There is a reason of principle involved, since only essential structures or relations were to be described. Thus, the Nazi revolution could only interest the phenomenologist as an example of revolution in general, which meant that he had nothing in particular to say about it *qua* phenomenologist. Husserl's way of looking at history, within the framework of his method as illustrated in his book on *The Crisis of the European Sciences and Transcendental Phenomenology,* has been discussed by the present writer.[1] It was Dr. A. Reinach, a disciple of Husserl in the latter's middle period, who attempted to apply the phenomenological procedure, as he conceived it, to social science and the philosophy of law.[2] The work of the late Professor Alfred Schuetz of the New School for Social Research in New York City may be cited as a recent attempt to apply phenomenological analysis to social science.[3]

Phenomenological description must be ordered under general description, as one among other modes of description. It has its successes for special problems, under carefully defined and restricted conditions. But it is incapable of handling other types of problem that require factual, naturalistic methods. The contention of some phenomenologists that the phenomenological procedure may not be subsumed under the general concept of "method," and that it is so radically different as to forbid reciprocal relations

[1] E. Husserl, *Die Krisis der europäischen Wissenschaften und die transzendentale Phänomenologie* (The Hague: Martinus Nijhoff, 1954). Cf. M. Farber, "Experience and Subjectivism," in *Philosophy for the Future,* edited by Sellars, McGill, and Farber (New York: The Macmillan Co., 1949).

[2] Cf. A. Reinach, "Die apriorischen Grundlagen des bürgerlichen Rechtes," in *Jahrbuch für Philosophie und phänomenologische Forschung,* vol. I, part II, edited by E. Husserl; and A. Reinach, *Gesammelte Schriften,* edited by H. Conrad-Martius (1921).

[3] Cf. A. Schuetz, "Phenomenology and the Social Sciences," in *Philosophical Essays in Memory of Edmund Husserl,* edited by M. Farber (Cambridge: Harvard University Press, 1940); and also his studies published in *Philosophy and Phenomenological Research,* XII, no. 2 (December, 1951) and XIV, no. 1 (September, 1953). Cf. A. Schuetz, *Collected Papers,* vol. I, *The Problem of Social Reality,* edited by M. Natanson (The Hague: Martinus Nijhoff, 1962).

with other procedures, is simply untenable. Husserl himself conceived of fruitful applications of phenomenological findings to empirical situations. On the other hand, the phenomenologist may try to begin without presuppositions, in the ordinary sense of the term, but he cannot hope to begin in complete ignorance. In fact, it would be unwarranted to assert that he does begin in ignorance. In short, the logical principle of the "cooperation of methods"[4] is appropriate, in place of the mistaken idea that phenomenology is absolutely detached from all general considerations of methodology.

The strict phenomenologist is not concerned with problems about the reality of the objects of experience, or with theories which try to show that we cannot pass beyond the immanent contents of consciousness. If I assert a judgment about the object before me, say the university library, the object is taken to be something transcendent of all "immanent" data. The judgment itself may be false, but it is certain that a transcendent thing, a building with a presumed place in the natural world, has been "perceived" or "judged" here. The phenomenologist is interested in that which is meant as such, and he maintains that it can be "grasped absolutely." Direct observation is the primary concern of phenomenology; and direct observation is held to be prior to all theory. Thus Husserl spoke of the finality of "seeing." That which is seen cannot be explained away, and is the final standard in all truly philosophical thought. The question of what is to be established as real or unreal as a matter of fact falls to empirical science or ordinary "natural" experience. Phenomenological questions belong to a different order, and begin with the reduction to pure conscious processes in experience. The nature of percep-

[4] Cf. M. Farber, *The Foundation of Phenomenology*, pp. 545, 569, 572.

tion, or of remembrance, or of other modes of experience, is the proper theme of phenomenological inquiry.

The descriptive analysis of meaning shows how broadly the concept of "seeing" is to be construed. Expression and meaning are essential to all knowledge, so that the analysis of meaning is one of the first themes of the critique of knowledge. We say that we use the *same* sign, or express the *same* meaning, at different times. If the Pythagorean theorem is asserted by two or more speakers, one may expect variations in the sound, just as variations in the written symbols may be expected. There will also be at least small physical differences in the expression if the statement is repeated. Hence if we say that the "same" signs have been used, we do not seem to be concerned with what happens as a matter of fact. The "same" signs, or the "same" meanings, belong to the "ideal" order. The sameness is "constituted" by experience; it is the result of a process of ideal identification. Ideal identifications are to be found everywhere in experience, and organized thought would be impossible without an accepted set of identifications. Such identifications are seen in the case of nonsensical or absurd expressions, as well as in logically acceptable examples. The proposition "π is a transcendental number" has ideally the same meaning in all of its repetitions. To ask whether an ideal meaning is real, would be to ask an improper question tantamount to asking whether something defined as ideal has a physical existence in space and time. The ideal meanings are "meant" objects, and they have their indispensable role to play in the course of experience. If one asks what they are in metaphysical terms, the answer can only be the reminder that they are non-real or ideal. On the other hand, the actual experiences referring to the "same" ideal unities are real.

It is necessary to extrude all metaphysics from the inquiry, in order to show the extent to which a purely

descriptive approach to philosophy is possible. Nothing
less than the full richness and complexity of experience is
to be considered. Husserl's talk of "ideal objects" has led
some superficial readers to criticize him for a "Platonic
hypostasis" of universals, and for reviving "Scholastic realism." He was right to defend himself against such charges,
for he could appeal to what occurs in ordinary experience.
One can see that the object of reference, the object meant
as the same in repeated experiences, is something objective
without being real. The necessity of dealing objectively
with ideal entities ("Ideas") in mathematics and logic
could be cited by Husserl as a cogent reply to the charge
of metaphysical dogmatism. The same mathematical proposition may be asserted countless times; the same symphony by Beethoven may be played again and again—but
it will probably never be the same real event in anyone's
experience, for objective as well as subjective reasons. Even
if the director and the musicians were to deliver an exact
performance according to a set standard, there are differences in atmospheric and acoustic conditions. One may
also expect differences on the part of the listener, for he
will be likely to "hear" the "same" thing differently the
second time—assuming that he really "heard" it the first
time! Neither is "the same" symphony to be identified with
any set of symbols, any more than it can be identified with
any one edition. The term "ideal" refers in a non-metaphysical way to this feature of sameness, which is universal in
our experience. The prominence in experience of "syntheses of identification" must be recognized, and it is important not to misconstrue that fact. To say that such
processes can be recognized descriptively is to warn against
a temptation to treat the "ideal" as superior to the changing
particular facts of experience. The extremes of Platonic
realism and nominalism must both be avoided, and the
phenomenologist, as a descriptive investigator of the struc-

tures of experience and knowledge, does not face the question whether there are really universals in existence. It is sufficient that identification is an important feature of conscious experience. "Existence," and all beliefs in it, as we have seen, have been "suspended"—not denied, but simply placed in abeyance so that description may proceed without prior commitments. It may then be ascertained how far we can proceed with evidence. It is important to consider the types of questions raised in phenomenology, so that the term "evidence" is not misunderstood. It is here taken to mean "self-givenness in experience."

This is all very fine if the program is carried out, and if the suspension of beliefs does not turn out to be the way to a metaphysics of immanent conscious experience. In that case, the "radical" procedure would result in a new dogmatism. Thus the reduction to pure consciousness must at all times serve the purposes for which it was instituted. It has its own proper questions, to be answered by descriptive analysis; and they are supposed to be non-metaphysical.

B. Essential Description and "General Seeing"

The realm of inquiry for phenomenology is that of *"ego cogito"* with its manifold *cogitata*, or experience and its objects as such. There is a stream of consciousness or experience, in which everything is a phenomenon. There is the man-phenomenon, animal-phenomenon, etc., corresponding to the *cogito*. One phenomenon is, for example, the same person given in a manifold of modes. If I wish to know what the conscious life of another ego is like, I must also regard the world as being given to him in appearances, and must try to take his place in his own mental life, to see things as he sees them essentially. In that case, I must

regard him as also making the phenomenological reduction in which he "suspends" my body and empirical subject, just as I had done for him.[5] Such considerations are
concerned with the general view of phenomena, and do
not as yet advance beyond the factual level, although we
have already indicated the course of the method.

Husserl has taken two decisive steps which are fundamental in his view: the transition (1) to essential or *eidetic*
inquiry, and (2) to "general seeing." The first-named,
eidetic view is meant to carry out the Platonic attempt,
and to prepare the way to metaphysics, although it need
not have anything to do with it at present. Brentano
opened up this field of investigation for Husserl, historically speaking, through his doctrine of intentional experience,[6] but he never adequately analyzed it. Husserl
regards intention as "sense-giving" (*Sinngebung*), with its
own laws (as in the *Logische Untersuchungen*). Consciousness must not be merely described; it must be apprehended
and described "eidetically" or essentially. Accordingly, one
does not begin with the fact of "*ego cogito*"; the factual
science of the "*ego cogito*" is suspended. Hume's investigation, which was based upon such a view, had led to skepticism. Husserl therefore regards a transcendentally based
science as alone being in a position to determine sense-data
and the world. In a sense that must be carefully examined,
an identity is said to persist throughout manifold experiences of an object. In what sense can it be said that in all
the transformations a thing may undergo, there persists
that which is not and may not be transformed? Whatever
persists in that way is held to be *essential* to the thing in

[5] Cf. L. Binswanger's paper "Über Phänomenologie," *Zeitschrift für die gesammte Neurologie und Psychiatrie*, LXXXII,
1923.

[6] Cf. F. Brentano, *Psychologie vom empirischen Standpunkt*
(1874).

question. The characteristic of being a spatial thing is essential to every thing. "Spatial thing in general" is therefore the highest region of things. One may in fantasy freely vary a thing, e.g., this table: it may be varied to be a bench or brick, but not to be a propositional function, if one does not wish to leave the universe of things. The most general essential character is, then, "spatial thing in general."[7] On the other hand, "conceivable object in general" would determine both the table and the propositional function. Things are here considered from the standpoint of *a priori* (pure) possibilities. Phenomenological description, as *essential* description, is held to be valid with unconditional necessity. The particular possibilities are apprehended in intuition purely as possibilities, and there is no assertion of real existence. In the freedom of fantasy one can deal with pure possibilities and, always *seeing*, gain that which is *general*.

This leads to (2) the general "seeing," to "seeing in general." Self-givenness (*Selbstgebung*) is the measure for everything. A thing may be *adequately* apprehended in "self-giving" perception, as a tone, for example. A melody on the other hand is spread out in time, so that it can never be apprehended as "originally" as a tone. It is in part perception and partly memory. Adequacy is the maximum self-givenness attainable. To apprehend something through intention is to know it by inspection. *Evidence* is the correlate of adequacy; clarity of seeing is here involved. There are degrees of evidence, all the way from complete fulfillment and apodictic judgments to disappointment and falsity. The fact that every person is likely to regard such a judgment as $2 + 2 = 4$ as "evident," as "intuitively" experienced, will not suffice for foundational purposes. The "original" meaning of evidence is self-givenness, having the

---

[7] This may be compared with Kant's pure forms of intuition.

meant object in view, as there "bodily." The concept of
evidence may be widened, to include probability and possibility, and in all cases there are the corresponding noetic
characters of degrees of adequacy and clarity of seeing.
To prove is to have insight, and this is seeing, which may
be clear and unclear. This is the locus of Husserl's doctrine
of *evidence*.[8] Husserl regards *seeing* as final: it spells having the thing itself and all questions come to an end at that
point. In deception or error there is a complex of having
the thing itself and not having it. The ideal is to have
adequacy.[9] Could it be said that the possibility of clear
seeing may not be disputed, since the denial refutes itself,
and that there can be clear seeing of unclear seeing? The
dialectical argument is not convincing as a matter of fact,
for it would be possible to have different degrees of unclearness, and even to experience unclearness with an
equal degree of unclearness. The term "seeing" may be
used in a very broad sense. Thus a Euclidean proposition
may be regarded as an object, in the sense that it can be
brought to self-givenness. That can be "seen" intuitively.
Although Euclid's proofs may be developed deductively, I
must "see," step by step. And it is an unwarranted demand
to ask for a foundation or proof of "seeing," for this is the
final test in methodology. It is the task of phenomenology
to describe essential generalities, to investigate the necessary types of consciousness with all its attendant possibilities. The essential necessities or *a priori* laws of consciousness must be delineated; and therewith the *cogitata,* as
fictions, contradictions, harmonious structures, true objects,

[8] Cf. E. Husserl, *Logische Unterschungen,* vol. II, pp. 549 ff.
[9] Cf. *Ideen,* pp. 126 f. The null-limit is darkness, the one-limit
is complete clarity, intuitiveness, or givenness. "Self-givenness"
must not, however, be identified with "original" or "bodily"
givenness, since it is a wider concept, including *"empty"* presentations, without being limited with respect to objects.

etc. To sum up: (1) there must be a descriptive analysis of essence; and (2) the corresponding "noetic" side of categorial intuition must be described.

C. Reduction and Constitution

It is wise to examine the procedure of phenomenology more closely at this point. If one begins with the stream of experiences of an individual person, under the defined conditions of the phenomenological "reduction," then "reality" is regarded as a correlate of experience. It corresponds to a mode of consciousness, just as probable being, doubtful being, or "null" being correspond to other modes of consciousness. In this view, the terms "truth" and "reality" have a meaning for us because of the structure of consciousness. Accordingly, we can only be assured of "real being" by a synthesis of verification in experience, and all adequate evidence for reality is said to be due to a synthesis that belongs to us. In short, reality has a "transcendental" foundation in us. Although the world is admittedly transcendent of consciousness, it is maintained by Husserl that every transcendent being is uniquely "constituted" in the life of consciousness, and is inseparably bound to this life. Consciousness, taken particularly as consciousness of the world, is held to carry in itself not only the unity of the meaning constituting this "world," but also "this world really existing." "Being an object really existing" means "being an identical object of actual or potential intentions in the unity of consciousnesss." The "real object" belongs to the world surely enough, but what is this world? The world itself is regarded as an "infinite idea," that involves infinities of harmonious experiences and is correlative to the idea of a complete synthesis of possible experiences. That reality is limited to its relation to experiencing beings is thus a fundamental principle of Husserl's procedure. It must then be shown how the meaning and structures of reality can be "constituted" in the processes of experience. The constructive program is indicated by the various provinces of "constitution," which include physical nature, human society, and culture. As a matter of method, Husserl is interested in examining the side of intentional (meaningful, referential) experience, to determine what it may reveal or imply.

The radical procedure of "suspension," outlined in his *Ideas*, was added to in his *Cartesian Meditations*. The natural world, physical and psychological, is suspended, as are all varieties of cultural expression, all works of the technical and fine arts, as well as of the sciences, and aesthetic and practical values of all kinds. The natural and cultural sciences, with the knowledge they have accumulated, are thus suspended as sciences that require the natural point of view for their development. Even formal logic and the entire field of the *mathesis universalis* are included in the process of suspension. The guiding precept is formulated as follows: to claim nothing that we cannot make evident by direct reference to consciousness, viewed immanently.

If the phenomenological reduction is carried out in an individual's consciousness to begin with, he must be careful to suspend all judgments based upon other human beings, or involving them. The phenomenological residuum becomes correspondingly narrower. What does it comprise? This is answered by a more precise application of the phenomenological method. With the natural point of view, I find myself in the world, along with other human beings. If I abstract from others, I am "alone." That which is peculiar to my ego is my concrete being as a "monad." For the purposes of the method, it is important to begin by extruding from the field of investigation not only the reality of others for me, but all modes of consciousness referring to what is strange to me, i.e., everything referring to "others," such as predicates expressing cultural values, for example.

In this way Husserl attempts to achieve the determination of a completely individual sphere of consciousness, proceeding with what is given in intuitive experience. Having eliminated all "strange" elements, there remains "the phenomenon of the world," as the transcendental correlate of the experience of the world. The sphere which comprises my own world represents the extreme limit attainable by phenomenological reduction. This is "first," and it must be attained in order to constitute the experience of "another ego distinct from me," which is necessary to make possible the "constitution" of an "objective world." If I proceed as a phenomenologist, I do not need the experience of an objective world or of another ego in order to have "my own world." That is shown by the radical completion of the method of "reduction," by which everything "strange" or "alien" to one's own conscious processes is suspended.

The ambiguity of the term "constitution" has been a source of difficulty. It should not be understood to mean the actual construction of the world, or of any part of it. In the context of a descriptive philosophy of pure experience, the "objective world" is treated as a meaning, as an "existence-sense." The point is to show how that meaning is "constituted" on the basis of my own "primordial world." There is also the level of constitution pertaining to another ego, or to other egos. Thus the sense of my "primordial world" is added to in such a way that it takes on the appearance of an "objective" world, a world that is the same for all knowers. It is the other ego that makes possible the "constitution" of an objective world of nature, comprising myself and all other egos. But, strictly speaking, the other ego, his subjective processes, and the set of appearances

he experiences, are not given in our experience "originally."
According to Husserl, the ego has a universe of its own,
which is reached by a descriptive analysis of his "apodictic
I am," by a process of "original self-explication." Within
this "original sphere" there is also a transcendent world.
This objective world is assured by an analysis of meaningful experience.

This shows how far Husserl has departed from the naturalistic view of temporal development in the elaboration
of his method. That "my own world," and the very conditions of my meaningful experience, presuppose other selves
and an objective world, which as a matter of fact can never
be eliminated, are facts genetically prior to the use of the
phenomenological method, and are not to be altered by the
adoption of that method.

It is imperative to "exhibit" or to show the reality of
other minds. A direct experience of another ego is ruled
out because it would then be nothing but a part of my
being to me. One seems to leave the deep level of my
"primordial world," in recognizing a "coexistence" that can
never be present "in person." The type of experience that
meets the need is an act which makes others "co-present,"
an act of apperception by analogy (or "analogical apperception") that Husserl calls "appresentation." The other
body resembles my own and leads me to conceive "analogi-
cally" that it is another organism. A sharp distinction is
drawn between apperceptions that pertain to the primordial sphere and those which appear with the meaning of
another ego, thus adding new meaning.

There still remains the constitution of humanity or of the
community. When Husserl speaks of the intentional analysis of the community, he has in mind the possibility of acts
of the ego which penetrate into other egos by means of the
experience of appresentation of other egos. Such acts "go
from me to you," and are the social acts necessary to estab-

lish the possibility of communication between human beings. In his view, it was an important problem to study these acts in their different forms and to clarify the essence of the social from the transcendental (or "radically reflective") point of view. Like Kant, he is concerned with pointing out the necessary presuppositions or conditions of an ordered process of experience, which is intended to include social experience. This approach carries with it the idealistic premise that the conditions of experience are also the conditions of a world of experience, the world being interpreted in terms of such experience. The different types of social community are portrayed as being constituted in the interior of the objective world, as spiritual objectivities *sui generis*. These communities are constituted in their various possible gradations, including personalities of a higher order.

Husserl's non-evolutionary standpoint is seen in his belief that the general empirical structure of the given objective world, including nature and culture, is to a great extent an "essential necessity." Phenomenology aims to clarify the essential laws that determine the manner in which the objective world "sinks its roots" into transcendental subjectivity, i.e., the laws that make the world comprehensible as a constituted meaning. "Existence" and "meaning of existence" are here used interchangeably, and despite the frequently expressed opposition to metaphysics, a new version of metaphysics is thus indicated. For phenomenology is antimetaphysical only in relation to the traditional forms.

In its positive program, it attempts the construction of *a priori* sciences on the basis of concrete intuition, including such sciences as pure grammar, pure logic, pure law, the eidetic science of the world as intuitively apprehended, etc. It is also interested in the elaboration of a general ontology of the objective world which embraces everything. This is metaphysics, in Husserl's view, if it is true that the ultimate knowledge of being may be called meta-physics. Rejecting the traditional metaphysics because of its speculative excesses, he sets up his own "apodictic" theory. Descriptions of experiences that "constitute" mean-ings and structures take the place of the physical reality, that is to say "eidetic" descriptions concerned with the essential nature of such experiences. It will be objected that "pure" subjectivity can yield nothing but itself, no matter how it may be treated. Husserl argues that although one's individual ego is alone absolutely certain, it cannot have experience of the world without being in communica-tion with other egos; it must be a member of a "society of monads." And a world in which communication is possible must be arranged in space and time. Furthermore, this is the only possible world. Not more than one world could be constituted, for it follows from the egological premise that a second world would not be compossible. As Husserl reasons, this one unique nature has to exist, if it is true that I carry in me structures implying the coexistence of other monads. The empty possibility exploited by solip-sists, that the entire realm of objective existence may be nothing but false appearance, is evidently ruled out. For Husserl, like Kant before him, wishes to allow for a world that will meet the needs and standards of scientific inquiry.

It is an important objective of phenomenology to give science a new and "higher" form. The task of "transcenden-tally constituting the world" (i.e., accounting for the world-meaning on the basis of a radical or pure type of reflection) is begun with the clarification of the meaning and "origin" of such concepts as world, nature, space, time, animal being, man, spirit, organism, social community, culture, etc. Would it be fair to state that these concepts, without being analyzed and clarified, serve as fundamental concepts in the positive sciences? To assert that they are to be engen-dered in phenomenology with a clearness and distinctness that does not admit of possible doubt is to make a bold claim. The analysis of basic concepts is always undergoing change in the special sciences, which cannot be said to be naïve or dogmatic in the hands of their ablest representatives. On the other hand, the phenomenological claim to superiority in the work of clarification can only be made good by exhibiting successfully accomplished facts in concrete examples. It must be admitted that this still largely remains to be done.

All the *a priori* sciences are regarded by Husserl as branches of the transcendental (purely reflective, or radically reflective) tree, the universal *a priori* being innate in transcendental subjectivity. Transcendental phenomenology, systematically and fully developed, is regarded as *eo ipso* a "universal ontology"; not a merely formal ontology, but one that contains all the possibilities of existence. This would be designed to provide the desired absolute foundation for the sciences.

Phenomenological psychology, which excludes everything touching psychophysiology, amounts to a transcendental type of metaphysics. It was Husserl's purpose to explain the intentional nature (the meaning-structure) of a spirit in general, and to project investigations that explain the intentionality constituted in this spirit. "First being," which sets the foundation for all that is objective in the world, is construed as transcendental intersubjectivity, or the totality of the monads. Husserl made the surprising statement that within this subjective sphere appear all the problems of contingent reality, such as death, destiny, and the "meaning" of history. It was his purpose to place such ethical and religious problems in the context within which every question must be placed that can have a possible meaning for us. This could not mean experience in the ordinary sense, of course, because in that case his contention would hardly be new. It will occur to many readers, no doubt, that historical problems are not to be handled by the phenomenological method, except in a very limited sense. Most of the historical problems are as remote from phenomenological analysis as death is. They have objective, "naturalistic" significance, and they cannot be reached from the pure ego, which is a thoroughly non-historical construction.

Husserl was proud to belong to the subjective tradition in philosophy, and to be able to deepen and extend it. He thought it was necessary first to lose the world by the method of "reduction," in order to find it later in the field of universal self-consciousness. Admittedly, there is merit in following him in the searching, relentless application of his method. Our vision is extended thereby, and our capacity for critical thought is increased. But one must be careful to recognize the limitations of this approach, and if he understands that the method is artificial and preparatory, he will hesitate before making any pretense to ontology. If philosophy is to be regarded as a "root-science," to use Husserl's words, it is also important that philosophy not forget its own "mother-earth," its actual, genetic foundation. In that case, it would never be able to "constitute" a world that would satisfy experience, i.e., our actual experience and factual knowledge. It must consider how any descriptive phenomenological findings could be said to legislate for reality. Could the analysis of conscious experience, even in the ideally finished form of a "geometry of experience," be said to condition the actual course of future experience, or the actual course of nature?

IV

Descartes and Husserl:
The Ideal of Certainty

A. Descartes and the Problem of Transcendence

That Husserl attached great importance to Descartes'
Meditations was shown by his repeated use of the Cartesian method of doubt as a means for introducing his method
of phenomenological reduction. One of his most characteristic and profound works—but also one of his most disputed
writings—was named in honor of Descartes, the *Cartesian
Meditations.* He regarded Descartes as initiating a new
epoch in philosophy. Although anticipated many centuries
before by St. Augustine in recognizing the "absolute evidence" of *ego cogito,* it was Descartes who made possible
the systematic use of that insight. The term "absolute"
means, among other things, the undeniable certainty of the
"*cogito,*" for to deny that I think would be to incur a contradiction; so the traditional argument goes. Husserl preferred to emphasize the way to subjectivism indicated by
Descartes in his *Meditations,* rather than the insights of
that great thinker into the deductive unity of scientific
knowledge and the nature of mathematical and scientific
method. Nor was it of interest to Husserl that Descartes'
dualistic metaphysics made it possible for him to achieve a

modus vivendi for the times, allowing the realm of physical substance to be subject to scientific determination, while providing for traditional philosophical and theological ideas in his theory of the mind and doctrine of innate ideas. It was the "pre-reduction" (i.e., pre-Husserlian) version of Descartes that interested Husserl; and it did not matter that Descartes was only too ready to abandon the quest of systematic doubt he had so winsomely undertaken. If the Descartes who emerges in Husserl's depiction takes on rather familiar phenomenological features, that is not surprising.

In Husserl's view, the philosopher can only begin by meditating, and the absoluteness of *ego cogito* must be maintained to provide the starting point for a transcendental philosophy. The much-discussed problem of the transcendence of consciousness results from the line of thought of Descartes' *Meditations*. The question is stated as follows: How is knowledge of the transcendent possible for us? Or, how is it possible that anything transcendent (or beyond consciousness) is knowable in consciousness?

If one follows Descartes in the procedure of doubting everything that can be doubted, then the world, other people, and my body are found to be subject to doubt. The doubting experience itself cannot be doubted, and with it, presumably, the doubting intelligence. The objects of men's experiences may not exist in truth; but the experiences themselves may not be doubted. Looking back at Descartes, Husserl remarked that he (Descartes) was not aware of the actual extent of his discovery of the pure experiences, nor that the field of an infinitely fruitful science had been gained, a science that would be fundamental in philosophy. But Descartes did not determine this field of consciousness "purely." That was reserved for Husserl. Pure consciousness, which is defined by means of the phenomenological reduction, may not be regarded as consciousness of the ego in the natural sense. The ego in this case is not a man in the world, for the man in the world must be suspended along with all bodily things. The world of nature and our beliefs in all existence are "put out of play"; they are suspended and "bracketed." Only pure consciousness remains, and that cannot be doubted. Since the "reduction" necessarily takes place in one's own ego, the beginning may be called the stage of "egology." In other words, as a matter of method the starting point of a "radical" philosophy, which aims to begin without assumptions about any kind of existence, is the stream of conscious experiences of an individual person. The "reduction," involving a "restriction," as it might be called, to one's own conscious experiences is merely the first stage of the method. As we have seen, in order to pass beyond the initial stage of what may be termed a "methodological" ("egological") solipsism, while retaining the strict requirements of phenomenological description, it was necessary to establish the reality of other egos. Although Husserl devoted considerable attention to this problem, his method has been regarded by many as inconclusive at this point. Inferences drawn from the similarity of the bodies of other persons to the existence of their minds are hardly "absolute" in character. The concept of "empathy" is not a solution. Some members of the phenomenological tendency have renounced the "egological" beginning and have begun with "intersubjectivity." In so doing, however, they have forfeited the unique value of a procedure which permits one kind of finality in the analysis of experience.

But does the Cartesian method of doubt really establish certainty? Even if Descartes' procedure is rendered consistent, and if the doubting is carried through as far as it will go, it can only certify the present doubting experience as indubitable. The doubt I had a moment ago, or the experience which I just had, have receded into the past, and it may be a trick of memory that they really occurred. If one takes the procedure of doubting seriously, he must not place absolute reliance on the memory; he is therefore confined to the experience he has now. But the "present" has already become "past," and it is no longer certain that it ever was a "present." A solipsism of the present, passing moment may be the outcome. One may have recourse to a general mind, or to a doctrine of fixed, essential structures which are "supertemporal," in order to extend the certainty of the present experience to a larger realm. In either case, however, there are special assumptions that would have to be proved applicable to the actual course of experience and the world. The procedure of doubt is really nugatory, so far as establishing an absolutely certain subjective realm is concerned. There is no possible way of avoiding the challenge of doubt, once the procedure is initiated; and the doubting applies equally to the subjective realm. One may indeed describe an essential structure, or an essential relationship, such as the backward reference of a memory to an original experience; but there is no absolute assurance, in a given case of remembrance, that one is not in error. This also applies to one's remembrance of having analyzed the structure of remembrance.

To be sure, the phenomenological method, involving the suspension of belief and "bracketing" of the objects of belief, is to be distinguished on principle from the Cartesian method of doubt, or from any version of that method. It is easy to read psychological requirements into the phenomenological procedure, and they do not belong here. But, this granted, any claim to "certainty," or any talk of the "apodictic," must be reconsidered.

On the other hand, the procedure of doubt cannot fail to be a liberating influence on one's thinking. If all things and beliefs are to be "questioned" for their evidence, it is well to begin with a universal suspension of beliefs, which is the analog of doubt in phenomenology, although with a positive aim. Having suspended all beliefs and assumptions, the phenomenologist has therewith defined a distinctive realm for inquiry—the realm of pure reflection. Every object in the world, whether natural or social, and every item of knowledge, is now viewed only as a correlate of a particular experience of an individual, reflecting person. The results of descriptive analysis by the reflecting phenomenologist are held to be such that they would be valid even if there were no actual human beings, or even if all human beings should disappear. For example, essential structures illustrated in perception, negation, intention and fulfillment in experience, etc., would remain valid as determinations of possible types of experience. While they are experienced, they are "certain"; and, like any mathematical proposition, they are valid no matter what the actual world is like.

Unfortunately for a philosophy operating within idealized structures, however, the real world of transcendent existence goes on regardless of the actual course of experience. Essential structures may remain fixed, but be devoid of application to the existing or cultural world. If new types of event emerge, there must be new concepts and essences. But if the ideal order is seen to be dependent upon the transcendent world of existence, the claims made for the advantages of the "inner" realm must be seriously qualified.

Husserl's aims are clearly revealed in his recently published book, *The Idea of Phenomenology*, which antedated his *Ideas* of 1913. He is here interested in achieving "an absolutely certain ground" in connection with Descartes' method of doubt, and he speaks of "the realm of absolute givenness." As he states it: "Every intellectual experience and every experience in general, in that it is executed, can be made to be the object of a pure seeing and grasping, and in this seeing it is an absolute givenness." It is not knowledge as a "psychological fact" that is to be explained; the natural conditions of knowledge are not to be investigated. It is rather the essence of knowledge and its claim to validity that must be clarified, i.e., brought to self-givenness.

If one adopts this method and ideal of knowledge, the problem of "transcendence" becomes a serious difficulty. For how can the experience get beyond itself? There is also the problem of how we can know anything which is not a content of experience. In the phenomenological critique of knowledge, one may not make use of any "pregiven" transcendence. If one does not understand *how* it is possible for knowledge to meet something transcendent of it, he also does not know *whether* it is possible. The line of thought is clear enough. In order to understand how knowledge of transcendence is possible, we must somehow "see" the relationship of knowledge to the object of knowledge. Since this is held to be impossible, we are to alter our course and perform the "reduction" to pure consciousness. No matter how certain one may feel that there are transcendent worlds, and no matter how high an opinion he may have of the natural sciences, he cannot "borrow" from them. All transcendence must be eliminated; the experience of all transcendences, whether I believe them or not, does not concern me here; they are "put out of play."

Unlike the pure experience or *cogitatio,* which is held to be absolutely given, the external world of outer perception is held to be problematical. As Husserl states it, "the transcendence of a thing requires that we place it in question. We do not understand how perception can meet something transcendent; but we do understand how perception can meet something immanent, in the form of reflective and pure immanent perception, of the reduced type." One may have an appearance in view which refers to, or means, something not given in the appearance itself, so that there may be doubt about its very being. But if the seeing itself is meant, and nothing but that which is grasped in seeing, then it does not make sense to doubt. This is regarded by Husserl as a finality, "an absolute self-evidence." As for that which is not self-evident, the problematical, he speaks of the "mystery" of transcendent meaning.

The philosophical consequences of Husserl's concept of transcendence are indicated when he asks about the evidence for the assumption of "things outside of me." Can they be assumed on the basis of outer perception? In Husserl's words, "A simple glance grasps my environment of things up to the furthest fixed stars. But perhaps that is all a dream, a sensory illusion." All that is given in a genuine sense is made up of various visual contents, apperceptions, and judgments. He concludes that the transcendent cannot be experienced on principle.

To ask about the existence of things "outside of me," as Husserl does, is to incur the danger of introducing a false abstraction, which may be called "the error of isolation." However, this would not be objectionable if it were recognized explicitly as artificial, for what it is and for what it can achieve. It is no objection to a method to point out that it operates under artificial conditions, so long as no attempt is made to ignore that fact, or to expect the artificial method to yield a metaphysics. This applies particularly to the subjectivistic approach of phenomenology. The possibility that the starry heavens might be a dream object, or an illusion, may be dismissed as of interest to philosophical neophytes alone. If the stars are dream objects, then so is the entire subjective realm, apart from the actual, direct content of a passing experience. The purported past experience may also be illusory, a trick of the memory. Thus one could not claim anything absolutely.

To speak, as Husserl does, of transcendence as a "contribution" of perception, and of evidence as a "psychical character," is to reveal an idealistic tendency. Certainly perception is of prime importance in the experience of transcendence. But the transcendence is there, and was there before perception, before all perceptions. It will be granted that evidence has a "psychical" aspect. But it requires the presence of the objectivity that is involved; hence it is more than a "psychical character." The "evidence" which is restricted to a "psychical character" can only be one aspect of evidence, or one type. The evidence of an expected eclipse of the sun involves the natural, "transcendent" world. It is no riddle that something—the physical objects—should correspond to the perception. The existence of transcendent objects is simply a fact, and the alleged epistemological riddle results from the artificial isolation of a realm of experiences from the events of the physical and social world. Furthermore, the notion of the "immediately given" may be misleading. What is "given," really? The term "given" is an unfortunate one in any case. There is the danger that it may be used assumptively, as though a mind exists in and by itself, to which something is "given." To state that the transcendent is not implied in the immanent is to incur the danger of a double error. In the first place, there can really be no such thing as "immanence," for there is no such thing as being "in the mind," whether it be Locke's "empty cabinet" or any other kind of long discarded receptacle. In the second place, to talk of immanence is justified only if it applies to a critical, reflective procedure, suspending existential beliefs and viewing everything "from the point of view of immanence," i.e., in "pure reflection." Such a strictly controlled, phenomenological procedure should not be exploited for the purposes of a "metaphysics of immanence."

B. Immanence and Transcendence

Knowledge and experience are always "of" something. But one does not *really* begin with pure experience (as though it could be disengaged from its natural setting!) and least of all with "evident" knowledge or "immediate givenness." The initial fact is a very big thing: the domain of nature and the cultural tradition. They are not "given" to or for a mind; they were there antecedently. The critique of knowledge must recognize the cognitive relation on the level of "outer" experiences, involving the knower and the known. It is unwarranted to begin by abstracting experience (the *cogitatio*), and then to find transcendence to be a riddle. The "riddle" evaporates when the assumptive character of the immanence–transcendence distinction is realized. It presents a "methodogenic" problem (a problem resulting from a method and its assumed construction), and the transcendentally based riddle disappears on naturalistic grounds. One must be careful not to inject into the naturalistic view a distinction proper to an opposing view. The *inductive* problem of inferring objects that are not immediately "given" should be distinguished from the pure (*abstractive*) epistemological problem, which involves an artificially isolated knower who is detached from all natural and cultural conditions. The pure ego of "immanent" consciousness is not a real being. The real knower is surely a natural event, with organic progenitors and a definite time of birth. He is indebted to the world and the social system for his survival, and for his standard of living, making reflective inquiry possible. He may nevertheless ask, in the course of his critical inquiry, for the evidence of an existing world and other knowers. Such questions must be justified by their special purposes, and by their results.

It can only be argued that the transcendent cannot be experienced on principle if the direct experience of an individual is meant, i.e., in one sense of the term "transcendence" implying something beyond my immediate field of experience. That is really the problem of inductive knowledge. If, however, the term "transcendence" names the objectivity meant in and by the experience, it is incorrect to say that the object of experience cannot be experienced. That would be to treat an artificial construction as though it were the total reality; and it would lead in turn to the conclusion that transcendent knowledge is impossible. If "pure" reflection, for which all belief in transcendent existence is suspended, comes up against this impasse, why not resort to a more complete type of reflection, which knows how to preserve all the findings of natural experience, and also how to value the special findings of "pure" reflection? The latter represents an important stage in philosophical method, but it is not the sole method of philosophy; to claim it as such would be to undertake the task of constructing all reality out of pure consciousness.

The dangers in the unguarded formulation of the phenomenological method which have been cited continue to be illustrated in Husserl's more mature writings. Thus, the absoluteness of a reflective experience is contrasted with the "accidental" nature of the existence of things. There is always the possibility that the further course of experience may require the abandonment of something previously established in experience. It may have been illusion, etc. But in the inner "absolute sphere" there is no place for conflict, mere appearance, or "being otherwise." Thus, the "thesis of the world," which is "accidental," is contrasted with the thesis of my pure ego and ego-life, which is "necessary" and "indubitable." Can one assent to the alleged "essential law" that "all bodily things can also not be, but no given inner experience can also not be"? If it is true that a series of sufficient causes produced a bodily given thing, how could it "not be"? That would contradict our knowledge of the nature of things. In practice, the fear of the "possibility" of hallucination, or of the deceptive power of some evil demon, is utterly empty. Husserl argues that no proofs derived from the empirical view of the world are conceivable that could assure us with certainty of the existence of the world. Doubt is held to be conceivable because the possibility of not being is not precluded. The terms "certainty" and "possibility" must be clarified in all relevant respects. "Certainty" *may* be taken to mean "incapable of being denied without contradiction"; and "possibility" may similarly have a narrow meaning, to the effect that anything is "possible" which does not involve contradiction. But there is also the meaning of "practical certainty," in the sense that "certain" means "certain enough." Is one "certain" that he has a home, or a place of employment? Let the exponent of a transcendental certainty doubt this at his peril. There is a place for formalism, or for fantasy; and there is an end to both of them. It is "logically" possible that the object before me does not exist, in the sense that there is no self-contradiction involved in the denial of its existence as the object of this particular experience. If it is considered as a member of the domain of physical objects, with their causal relations, it is not "possible" to deny its existence, or its occurrence, because that would be to disagree with (to "contradict" in a broader sense) the known order of nature. For the rest, it must be emphasized that if one is allowed to look at an object and to say, "there is no such thing," he is hardly better off in the subjective realm, where he may be "certain" while he has an experience that he has it, but cannot be certain that he just had it. In other words, he is sure that it *is* while it is, but he is not at all sure that it *was*.

That Husserl has prepared the setting for a species of philosophical idealism is seen when he correlates the real world and consciousness. He admonishes his readers not to allow themselves to be deceived by the talk of the transcendence of a thing as opposed to consciousness, or by its "being-in-itself." That he does not stop short of idealism is seen again in his declaration that consciousness and the conscious ego refer to every object "which is in itself." "If there are worlds at all," he writes, "real things, then the experiential motivations *constituting* them must be able to reach into my experience, and the experience of every ego." And yet, Husserl muses, returning to his transcendental method, it is not said with all this that there *must* be a world at all. The existence of a world is in his view "the correlate of certain manifolds of experience, distinguished by certain essential formations." Thinking of "the possibility of non-being which lies in the essence of every thing-ish transcendence," it appears to him that "the being of consciousness, of every stream of experience in general, is indeed necessarily modified by a 'nullification' (*Vernichtung*) of the thing-world, but is not disturbed in its own existence." Husserl's choice of the term "nullification" is unfortunate. In the present context, "nullification of the world says correlatively that in every stream of experience . . . certain ordered connections of experience . . . are excluded. . . ." No real being, he holds, "no kind of being which is represented through appearances, is necessary for the being of consciousness itself, in the widest sense of a stream of experience." Thus, "immanent being" is "absolute being." On the other hand, the world of the transcendent "*res*" or things is held to involve actual consciousness and not merely a logically conceived consciousness.

This is expressed pointedly with regard to the initial

stage of the phenomenological reduction in Husserl's recently published *Pariser Vorträge*.[1] That an object exists for me, is taken to mean that it is valid for me in accordance with consciousness. On the "egological ground" of the phenomenologist, existence and determinate being have the meaning of "being on the basis of possible confirmation." True being, whether real or ideal, has meaning only as a particular correlate of my own intentionality.

Husserl's transcendental argument is expressed most systematically in his *Ideas*. Something transcendent is said to be "given" through certain connections of experience. But there is a fundamental difference between "immanent or absolute being" and "transcendent being." Both are said to "be" and to be "objects." It is urged, however, that a true abyss of meaning separates them. The transcendent being is never given completely, and is merely accidental and relative being; whereas the immanent realm is necessary and absolute being. One could say that the incompleteness of natural experience is given completely in reflective experience. With the suspension of all judgments of existence through the phenomenological reduction, nothing is really lost, Husserl maintains, and the entire region of "absolute being" is gained, a region which harbors all worldly transcendences in itself, and "constitutes" them. The program of a transcendental, constitutive phenomenology is thus indicated.

With the natural "point of view" or "attitude" (*Einstellung*), we are said to perform "all the acts through which the world is there for us." We are said to live "naïvely" in perceiving and experiencing. With the phenomenological "point of view," instead of "living in" the experiences, acts

[1] Cf. E. Husserl, *Cartesianische Meditationen und Pariser Vorträge*, edited by S. Strasser (The Hague: Martinus Nijhoff, 1950), pp. 23 ff.

of reflection are directed upon them, and they are apprehended as "absolute being." This "infinite field of absolute experiences" is the realm of phenomenological inquiry. The realm of "pure consciousness" which is achieved by the "radical reflection" is not a part of nature, according to Husserl, because nature is only possible as an intentional unity motivated in the realm of consciousness through immanent connections. Nature cannot be presupposed as a premise, because the transcendental view requires that nature be "bracketed on principle." Such an argument goes too far, however. It is not necessary for the phenomenologist to deny that events, whether "inner" or "outer," have a locus in physical reality, in time and space. It is enough to recognize that no use is made, *in such inquiry*, of the thesis of existence, or of naturalistic explanatory principles. If the phenomenologist is not bereft of all good methodological sense, he knows very well that the findings and procedures of the natural sciences always remain valid from a more general methodological point of view than he requires for his work.

The primacy and autonomy of the ego and its life are again discussed by Husserl in his *Cartesian Meditations*. As he states it there, I and my life remain undisturbed in my "validity of being" no matter what happens to the world by way of being or non-being, no matter how I may decide about that. The ego and ego-life remaining after the suspension of beliefs (the *epoché*) "is not a piece of the world, and if it says: 'I am, *ego cogito*,' that no longer means: I, this man, am." Husserl's assumption in the course of his reasoning may be held up to view. If I suspend all beliefs concerning a transcendent world, my inner experiences of the presumed world cannot be said to have a locus in the world. Furthermore, if all scientific judgments based on the realm of nature are placed in abeyance, the residual ego cannot be the objectively determined self of anthropology and naturalistic psychology; and we must also get away from biology, including physiology. This is not to say that the phenomenologist really suspends physiological processes—breathing, digestion, etc., or that he is not dependent upon the physical universe for his natural existence. That would be to forget the specialized nature of phenomenological questions. The natural order and the artificial order of pure, "reduced" experience should not be confused. The phenomenological reduction should be viewed as a device of method, and evaluated by its success in adding to human knowledge, as well as in solving problems in its own realm.

A problem-situation and a goal are always inherent in the use of a method. In the case of phenomenology, there is the alleged unsatisfactoriness of natural perception, the contention that it is impossible to construct a satisfactory philosophy on the basis of the sciences, the argument that we should not "presuppose" transcendent facts, on the one hand; and there is the positive desire for certainty, absoluteness, and completeness, on the other hand. These considerations lead to the methodological isolation of the knowing self, and to a beginning with artificially detached experiences (the *cogitationes*). As a matter of fact, however, there can be no isolated self, there can be no pure experiences without their causal conditions, no mind without a body, or without a brain, and no survival without the natural ("transcendent") world that comprises it. An outer perception cannot be treated apart from the stimulus, and an inner perception similarly involves causal conditions as well as the meant object. It must always be borne in mind that one merely *suspends* beliefs, or existential theses, in performing the reduction to pure consciousness, in order to make possible a more thoroughgoing reflective inspection of the process, structure, and validity of knowledge. One must make sure that there is no tacit assumption of a metaphysics from the outset. With appropriate assumptions, beginning with the depreciation of the naturalistic-scientific view of the world and its methodology, one may be committed to a "supertemporal," eternalistic view. This question is unfortunately only too fair, as proved by Husserl's further development of his method, and it is all the more important in view of some of the recent developments known as "philosophies of existence," some of which have gone all the way to irrationalism and fideism.

V

Phenomenological Description and the Limits of Pure Reflection

A. The Function of Phenomenology

Husserl distinguishes the phenomenological reduction carefully from the restriction of judgments in the various sciences of reality. For example, physics "abstracts" from psychological facts on the basis of the one "nature." It is entirely different with the realm of experiences as "absolute essences." This realm is said to be "closed in itself, and yet without limits, which could separate it from other regions." That which could delimit it would have to have something essential in common with it. Thus, like Spinoza's substance, this "all of absolute being" stands alone. Because it is *essentially* independent of all mundane, natural being, Husserl concludes that it does not require the natural world for its *existence*. He declares that the existence of a natural world cannot condition the existence of consciousness, since the world is itself the correlate of consciousness, "it *is* only as constituting itself in ordered contexts of consciousness." This contention is hard to reconcile with the avowed descriptive purpose of the phenomenological reduction. It can only be maintained with the tacit assumption of the cardinal principle of idealism, which makes "being" dependent upon "being experienced."

It turns out that Husserl is not disposed to grant the validity of the issues of "idealism" and "realism." This is made evident in the course of his discussion of the "reduction." Thus, he states that "real unities" are "unities of meaning." He maintains that he is not deducing anything from metaphysical postulates, and insists that he can justify his contention intuitively and beyond all doubt. In his view, "unities of meaning" presuppose a consciousness that gives the meaning, and this consciousness is for its part absolute and is not itself indebted to anything else. The drift of his argument is again antinaturalistic, when he states: "If one draws the concept of reality from the *natural* realities, then 'world-all,' 'All of nature,' is to be sure as much as the All of the realities, but to identify this with the All of *being*, and to absolutize it therewith, is absurd." Husserl does not justify his contention that there would be a contradiction in the position that nature comprises all reality or being. Only an appropriately defined "being" which goes beyond nature in some way could cause any difficulty—and it would simply stand as a definition. Husserl challenges the conception of an "absolute reality," which is, in his view, no more valid than the conception of a round square. "Reality" and "world" are for him simply "a title for certain valid *unities of meaning*, . . . related to certain connections of the absolute, pure consciousness, which are essentially meaning-endowing in a certain way, and not otherwise."

To the possible charge that he has lapsed into a Berkeleyan idealism (like Berkeley himself!), Husserl retorts brusquely that the meaning of his presentation would be misunderstood therewith. "Reality" is not "transformed" or denied; rather, "an absurd interpretation of it which contradicts its own meaning" is obviated. If one seeks final knowledge about the meaning of the world, he would not, in Husserl's words, fail to realize "that the world itself has its entire being as a certain 'meaning' which presupposes absolute consciousness as the field of meaning-endowment." But, as already noted, this contention is neither clarified nor justified. The field of "absolute consciousness" is called the "being-sphere of absolute origins," a sphere that is open to descriptive inquiry, and capable of yielding endless results of the highest scientific dignity.

Nowhere is this claim more strongly supported than in the elucidations and "origin-analyses" of logical forms provided by Husserl's great trilogy of logical studies—his *Logical Investigations, Formal and Transcendental Logic,* and *Experience and Judgment.* The occurrence of paradoxes in formal logic has usually been met by technical solutions. Husserl proposed to clarify formal logic by a thoroughgoing constructive attempt, beginning with the careful analysis of basic ideas and principles. His point was that paradoxes should be rendered impossible by means of a well-founded logic, rather than by means of subsequent patchwork. All logical ideas and forms were accordingly to be traced back to their "origin" in experience. This is not meant to be a historical study of "origins" in the usual sense of the term, but rather an account of the formation of complex structures out of ultimately simple elements. The descriptive analysis of the level of receptive experience, which is the lowest stage of the activity of the ego, shows the origin of such ideas as negation, relation, and possibility to be in "pre-predicative" experience. The "original phenomenon of negation" is described as a phenomenon of "annulment." It is conveniently illustrated by means of outer perception, but can also be shown in all cases of "positional" consciousness. Negation is not primarily a matter of predicative judgment; it already appears in its "primal" form on the more rudimentary level of receptive experience. It can be *seen* how belief conflicts with belief. The conflict consists in the peculiar "annulment" of an anticipatory intention, an expectation through a new impression, which is called "disappointment." Consider an example in which disappointment enters in, instead of the fulfillment of an intention. Suppose that an object appearing to be a uniformly red sphere is seen. For a time the course of perception is such that this apprehension is harmoniously fulfilled. Then, when one gets to the other side, he notes that it is not red, but green. There is a conflict between the still living intentions and the sense-contents now appearing. The new objective sense "green" in its impressional power of fulfillment has "certainty in primal force," which overcomes the certainty of the "pre-expectation" of red. "Negation" is described as a modification of consciousness, as a partial "crossing-out" on the ground of a certainty of belief, ultimately on the ground of the universal world-belief. "Doubt" as a mode of consciousness is regarded as a transitional "modus" to the negating annulment. The consciousness of possibility and other types of experience is similarly described. Thus, problematical possibility arises out of a situation of doubt, and is contrasted with *open* possibility, which is founded on the uninhibited course of perception.

In the course of his attempt to clarify the nature of logic and its sources in experience, Husserl indicates his acceptance of idealism as a philosophy. This occurs in one of his most mature, and certainly one of his most important works, the *Formal and Transcendental Logic*. The psychologism, or the logical psychologism, which he had rejected early in his career is replaced by a "transcendental psychologism" in his later work. Despite the general acclaim accorded to the early critique of psychologism on the publication of the *Logical Investigations*, it would now be timely to reexamine the entire case against that much criticized position. Hussserl has been credited so often with having given a full and fair hearing to the exponents of logical psychologism that a reappraisal has been generally regarded as unnecessary. The question whether faulty defenses of a naturalistic and empirical philosophy of logic could be corrected and replaced by a more adequate view remains to be answered in connection with Husserl's work. This must be undertaken in the light of a pluralistic conception of method, and on the basis of an ontology that does justice to the facts of experience and knowledge.[2]

The reconsideration of Husserl's arguments will determine whether Husserl went too far in his opposition to naturalistic philosophies. It will also show whether the concept of "essence" has been sufficiently clarified, despite the repeated statement that phenomenology is throughout a science of essences and essential laws. The relationship of essences to the events and facts of the natural world must be made clear, first of all; one cannot ask about the essence of war, or the essence of property, before the natural world has developed the requisite events. This is not an argument against the justification for a pure phenomenology of experience and its objects. It is, however, a warning that such a pure phenomenology cannot be self-sufficient, either as a descriptive method, or as a way to an ontology and a general philosophy. What is required is the *cooperation* of all methods that can be justified logically.

B. Time-Consciousness

In his analysis of experience, Husserl was led to devote considerable attention to the consciousness of time,[3] which

[2] Cf. the present writer's *Naturalism and Subjectivism* (1959).

[3] Cf. E. Husserl, *Vorlesungen zur Phänomenologie des inneren Zeitbewusstseins*, edited by M. Heidegger (Halle: Max Niemeyer, 1928). Cf. the present writer's "Review of Recent Phenomenological Literature," *Journal of Philosophy*, XXVII (1930).

he regarded as the first and basic form, and as the presupposition of all connections which establish unity. The real world is not a phenomenological datum, and neither is the time of nature in the sense of natural science, or of the natural science of psychology. When Husserl speaks of the descriptive analysis of time-consciousness, or of the temporal character of the objects of experience, he does not mean to assume objective time. He is concerned with *appearing* time and *appearing* duration as such, and he does not assume the existence of a world time. The appearing time and duration are regarded as being absolutely given, in the sense that doubting them would be meaningless. The external appearances may or may not exist in truth, but the appearances themselves are indubitable. The existing time that is assumed in the realm of appearances is the immanent time of the stream of consciousness. There is thus an essential change from the contingent realm of transcendence to the "certain" realm of immanence. The evidence that we have for the fact that the consciousness of a tone or melody exhibits a succession is given as an example of inner certainty. It is such that all doubt or denial would be meaningless. This distinguishes the phenomenological field for description, with its suspension of all judgments of transcendent existence. Objective space and time, and the world of real things and events, are transcendent entities which are "bracketed" in order to make possible a descriptive science of pure immanence.

The phenomenological approach to the problem of time is thus distinguished from the psychological approach. The phenomenologist is interested in a study of the "origin" of time, i.e., the "primitive formations" of time-consciousness. He is not concerned with the pyschological problem of the origin of time, or with the way in which objective space and time perception arise in the human individual or species. The question of the empirical origin of time is a matter of indifference to him. The content and objective meaning of pure experiences are the theme for his descriptive analysis. These experiences are not fitted into any "reality." Reality concerns him only insofar as it is meant, perceived, or conceived. With regard to the problem of time, this means that temporal experiences interest the phenomenologist. It is important for him that "objective temporal" data are *meant* in these experiences. The description of the way in which cognitive acts mean this or that "objectivity," or, more specifically, the determination of the "*a priori* truths" which govern the "constitutive factors of objectivity," belong to the task of phenomenology. Husserl endeavors to delineate this *a priori* nature of time by investigating time-consciousness and determining its essential structure. His investigation takes account of the specific contents of temporal experience as well as the acts through which they arise. By the essential structure of time, he means laws such as the following: That the fixed temporal order is that of an infinite series; that two different times can never be at the same time; that the relational nature of time is insymmetrical; that it is transitive; that to every time there belongs an earlier and a later stage, etc.

It becomes evident that a complete descriptive analysis of the process of experience, and particularly of the acts of knowledge through which objects are given, must be undertaken in order to achieve an adequate theory of time. Husserl asks how we are to explain the apprehension of transcendent time-objects, whether changing or changeless, which are extended over a duration. Such objects are said to be "constituted" in a manifold of immanent data and views, which occur as a succession. Is it possible to unite these successively occurring representative data in a present experience? An entirely new question now arises. How, along with the temporal objects, both immanent and transcendent, is time itself constituted; how are the duration and succession of objects constituted? It is evident that the perception of duration presupposes the duration of perception, and that the perception of any time-form has its own time-form. If we abstract from all transcendences, then only phenomenological time remains. Husserl goes beyond description and reveals a metaphysical tendency when he states that "objective time is actually constituted phenomenologically" and that "it is there for us as an objectivity and as an element of an objectivity only through this constitution." Phenomenological analysis therefore must undertake an account of the constitution of time-objects.

Let us follow Husserl in a typical example of his descriptive analysis in this context. With a few changes in its vocabulary, there would be no suggestion of metaphysical implications. Suppose that a time-object, a tone, for example, is viewed as a pure sense-datum. It begins and stops, and the unity of the entire occurrence recedes into the ever more remote past. In the recession I still have a "hold" on it, I have it in retention; and as long as the retention lasts the tone has its own time, it is the same, its duration is the same. I can attend to its aspect of givenness. It and the duration it fills are known in a continuity of "modes," in a "continuous stream." The tone is given—i.e., it is known "now"; and it is known as now so long as any one of its phases is known as now. But if any phase of time, with the exception of the beginning phase, is a present now, then a continuity of phases is known as "before," and the entire stretch of the time-duration from the beginning point until the now-point is known as a past duration; but the remaining stretch of the duration is not yet known. At the close the end-point is itself known as a now-point, and the entire duration is known as "past." "During" this whole stream of consciousness the one and the same tone is known as "enduring," as enduring "now." It was not known "before," in case it had not been expected; and it is "still known" for a time "afterwards" in retention, in which it can be fixated and remain as past. The entire stretch of the duration of the time or "the" time in its extension remains then as something "dead," with no creative point of the now to animate it; but it is continually modified and lapses back into "emptiness."

What has been described is the whole in which the immanent temporal object "appears" in a continuous stream, in which it is "given." However, to describe this mode is not the same as to describe the appearing time-duration itself. For the same tone with the duration belonging to it was not described but rather presupposed in the description. The same duration is a duration now being built up, which then becomes a "past" duration: it is still known and is formed anew "as it were" in memory. The tone which now sounds is the same tone which is viewed as past in a later stream of consciousness. The points of time-duration remove themselves from my consciousness analogous to the way in which the points of a resting object in space are removed from me when "I remove myself from the object." The object keeps its place, and similarly the tone keeps its time; every time-point is changeless, but it flees to the remotenesses of consciousness, and the distance from the creative now becomes ever greater. The tone itself is the same, but the tone "in the mode how" ("*in der Weise wie*") appears always as a different one.

Husserl showed great skill in finding complexity where others see only simplicity, and in this respect he did indeed extend the vision of philosophy. There is a difference, for example, between the modification of consciousness which transforms an original now into a reproduced now, and the modification which transforms either an original or reproduced now into a past now. The latter passes by continuous gradations into the past; whereas there can be no talk of a continuous transition from perception to fantasy, or from impression to reproduction.

The sphere of time-consciousness is finally divided into three levels, or "stages of constitution," the last stage being that of the absolute stream of consciousness which constitutes time. Subjective time is regarded as constituted in an absolute "timeless" consciousness, which cannot be an object of cognition. This absolute consciousness is supposed to be prior to all constitution. The "absolute subjectivity" to which Husserl finally has recourse is held to be the most fundamental principle of experience, which defines at the same time a necessary condition for *objects* of experience. On the basis of this principle, the emergence of all objects, including transcendent objects and things, is to be explained. That temporal things are "constituted" and are as such dependent upon an absolute subjectivity, and that, furthermore, spatial things are constituted similarly, since they are held to presuppose a temporal constitution, clearly indicates a standpoint of genetic, transcendental idealism. Fortunately, Husserl's descriptive results may stand independently of such systematic philosophical use.

The very formulation of the problem of the constitution of objectivity in subjectivity indicates a metaphysical preference. That the stream of experience occurs in configurations, that cognitive contents are formed as unities amid multiplicity, may be taken as matters of fact, whether viewed empirically or phenomenologically. Furthermore, that experiences are "intentional," and so refer to objects "of" which they are experiences, is an important principle for Husserl. But the objects themselves are not "constituted" phenomenologically. The alleged constitution occurs only on the cognitive side, and it would be sheer dogmatism to inject such a condition into the essence of objectivity. The phenomenological method is *per se* unable to restore the external world to its position of stability and independence, however far from "absoluteness" it may be from the natural point of view. The material realm of existence must be recognized as the basic fact for the world of experience, and no theory of reality can afford to dispense with it.

The phenomenological method is basically a reflective procedure. But it is evident that Husserl did not succeed in reflecting fully upon himself. That would have required a more complete reflective view than he had at his disposal. To reflect about reflecting, and so on *ad infinitum*, need not yield any new results, i.e., beyond the stage of reflecting about reflecting to make sure that the phenomenologist has been faithful in following out his own precepts. A *complete* reflective procedure must recover the natural and cultural "dimensions" of inquiry, in addition to the phenomenological "dimension"; and the phenomenologist is seen as historically conditioned. Thus, Husserl might have been able, finally, to see himself as dismissing Berkeleyan idealism, while being nevertheless tacitly inclined toward assuming the cardinal principle of idealism by way of correlating existence and consciousness. From the perspective of a more general methodology, it could be seen how he mistook his own view of the "constitution" of reality in conscious experience for the reality based upon the existence of the physical universe. A more complete reflection would be extended to include the knower as a body, as a human being in a social system, and as historically conditioned. It would then be seen why numerous scholars manifested an antiscientific feeling, or opposition to a philosophy based upon the sciences. The motives for such opposition are usually moral or religious, but they may also be political. The ideal of absolute certainty, and the aim to "overcome" time, are served by means of the restriction to pure experience, and the use of "essential" analysis. With the more complete reflective view, Husserl himself could be seen as an admirer of the First *Reich,* and as a person who was willing to accept historically conditioned class distinctions. Despite these observations, however, it may be recognized that there is merit in carrying through the "radical" suspension of all beliefs. That is an indispensable stage in philosophical thought. It not only leads to the domain of inquiry in phenomenology, but also helps to achieve the openmindedness and basic understanding necessary for philosophy. The important thing to bear in mind, however, is that phenomenology must be construed as a descriptive procedure, and as subordinated to general methodology. It must not be allowed to operate from tacit metaphysical premises.

C. Phenomenology and Psychology

Although he was critical of naturalism as a philosophy, and although he repeatedly insisted upon pointing out the limitations of the scientific psychology of his time, Husserl did not wish to be thought of as antipsychological. He was opposed to overextending the factual science of psychology by making it serve as a foundation for philosophy. As for phenomenology, it was to serve as an aid to empirical psychology. It was also a basic part of his program to develop a pure descriptive psychology as an integral part of the general essential science of phenomenology, i.e., as a discipline exclusively devoted to essential relations and laws.

The relationship between phenomenology and psychology was discussed at some length in Husserl's *Logos* essay,

"Philosophy as a Rigorous Science,"[4] as well as in numerous published books and unpublished manuscripts. It remained one of his major themes throughout his scholarly life. In the *Logos* essay, Husserl's antinaturalistic motivation takes the form of an attack on the philosophical potentialities of the sciences of nature. As he states it, "to exercise radical criticism of the naturalistic philosophy is nowadays an important matter." He undertakes to expose the weakness and untenableness of "naturalistic philosophy." The question of the status of scientific philosophy was crucial at the time, and Husserl was concerned with circumscribing its validity and extent, and with instating "pure" ("eidetic") psychology as a necessary foundation for empirical psychology.

All the natural sciences were regarded by Husserl as "naïve" in their point of departure. The realm of nature which natural science investigates is taken to be simply "there" for it. There are things in infinite space and time that we perceive and describe. This holds for psychology as well. The natural science of psychology has the task of investigating psychical facts in the psychophysical context of nature. The important point is that all the events investigated by naturalistic or empirical psychology are regarded as belonging to nature, to human or animal consciousness. This applies also to psychology conceived as the science of experience, for the conscious events with which it is concerned are included in the realm of nature. If the relationship to nature were suspended, the character of being a psychological fact would be removed.

It is interesting to note how Husserl emphasized the "naïveté" with which natural science takes over nature as

[4] E. Husserl, "Philosophie als strenge Wissenschaft," *Logos*, vol. I (1911); and cf. the present writer's *Naturalism and Subjectivism*, chap. VI.

"given," a "naïveté" which he declared to be "immortal" in it. He conceded that natural science is very critical in its way. But, he argued, it is necessary to undertake a critique of experience which places in question *all* experience, and all empirical-scientific thinking. And this applied to psychology as well as to physical science.

Husserl's aim was to institute a new science, the enormous extent of which his contemporaries had no idea. It was, to be sure, a science of consciousness, and yet it was not psychology. It was a "phenomenology of consciousness" as opposed to a natural science of consciousness. He made it clear that phenomenology and psychology must stand in very close relationship since both are concerned with consciousness, even though in a different manner, and from a different point of view. Psychology is concerned with empirical consciousness, as something existing in the context of nature, whereas phenomenology is concerned with "pure" consciousness, from a specially defined point of view. It follows that psychology can no more be philosophy than physical natural science can, even though it is closer to philosophy for essential as well as historical reasons. But Husserl did not wish this to be understood to apply to modern exact psychology. He disputed its claim to be the psychological science, and this was taken to apply emphatically to experimental psychology. In his view, experimental psychology is related to "originary" psychology rather as social statistics is related to "originary" social science. Social statistics may indeed gather valuable facts and discover valuable regularities in them, but they are of a very indirect kind. Their understanding and real explanation can only be accomplished by an "originary" social science, or a social science which brings the sociological phenomena to direct givenness and investigates their essence. Similarly, experimental psychology establishes psychophysical facts and regularities. However, the question is whether it can achieve a deeper understanding without a systematic, immanent science of consciousness. The experimental method is admitted to be indispensable for the determination of intersubjective connections of facts; but it is held by Husserl to presuppose something that no experiment can contribute—the analysis of consciousness itself.

All three volumes of Husserl's *Ideas,* which are now available in published form, contribute methodological discussions on this theme. Two questions must be borne in mind: whether a descriptive, essential science of pure consciousness has been satisfactorily established; and whether phenomenological essential findings may be applied fruitfully to situations in empirical psychology. It may well be that insights and formulations contained in Husserl's writings will prove to have valuable application to factual situations. Among these writings, *Experience and Judgment* has not yet received the attention it deserves on the part of psychologists and philosophers, and his descriptive studies of "time-consciousness" should be called to the attention of students of psychology, along with the recently published book on *Phenomenological Psychology.*

It is an interesting fact that phenomenology found a far more receptive field immediately in its application to psychiatry. Professor Karl Jaspers was one of the forerunners in this movement. An extensive literature has resulted, and phenomenological psychiatry is now a widely known method of approach. Dr. J. H. Van den Berg, professor of psychology at Leyden University, Holland, and himself a phenomenological psychiatrist, has recently published a book[5] which reviews this literature. Brentano and Husserl

[5] *The Phenomenological Approach to Psychiatry* (Springfield, Illinois: Charles C. Thomas, 1955). Among recent publications on phenomenology and psychology, mention may be

figure prominently as influences. The later influence of
Heidegger is seen in the direction taken by the Swiss psychiatrist, Dr. L. Binswanger, among others. The "inner" approach" of phenomenology is a favorable device for recon-
structing and evaluating the meaning-world of the patient.

Mention should also be made of Husserl's conception of
a "pregiven" life-world, first presented in published form
near the close of his life. It will be borne in mind that the
natural view of the world had been "suspended," as a first
stage in the procedure of phenomenology. The objective
world "constituted," after much descriptive analysis, re-
places with "certainty" a "contingent" realm of existence
that does not have to exist. With this "constitutive" outcome, why was it necessary to introduce the conception of
a life-world, and to acknowledge that it is "pregiven"?
It is not to be supposed that Hussserl renounced the basic
thesis and program of his constitutive phenomenology, according to which all concepts, meanings, and structures are
to be traced back to their "origins" in simpler forms of experience. It can only be concluded that his thought system
was left incomplete, and that a partial concession to other
methods and approaches remained indeterminate. The
widespread interest in the concept of the life-world was
evidence of the desire to go beyond the subjective realm,
at least in Husserl's rigorous sense of pure subjectivity.

made of M. Merleau-Ponty's *Phénoménologie de la Perception*
(Paris: Librairie Gallimard, 1945); English trans. by Colin
Smith, *Phenomenology of Perception* (New York: Humanities
Press, 1962); the symposium on Phenomenology and Psychology in *Philosophy and Phenomenological Research,* VII, no. 3
(March, 1947); and A. Gurwitsch's "The Phenomenological
and the Psychological Approach to Consciousness," *Philosophy
and Phenomenological Research,* XV, no. 3 (March, 1955), and
his *The Field of Consciousness* (Pittsburgh: Duquesne University Press, 1964).

Various philosophers, including idealists like Hocking and existentialists like Heidegger, professed to begin with an intersubjective realm, with a society of experiencing persons. But the term "existence" becomes as puzzling in its way as the terms "subjectivity" and "transcendence" had been. The old alignment of standpoints remains: there are subjective and objective versions of "existence." Husserl's "life-world" has at least, and presumably at most, a provisional status, so far as its "pregivenness" is concerned. It was there always, he acknowledges. But the "being there always" is taken to be meaningful only in relation to a human knower. In the last analysis, it is subjectivism that triumphs in Husserl's system of thought.[6]

[6] Cf. the present writer's forthcoming book on *Phenomenology and Existence* (New York: Harper & Row), for a fuller discussion of the "life-world."

VI

The Object of Experience
for Phenomenology

A. Act, Content, and Object

It is a general question for philosophy to determine the object of knowledge: in a sense, everything is or can be made an object of knowledge. Thus, there are the so-called "things," tones, creaking noises, words; ideal objects, such as the propositions of mathematics; and social objects. Or, to put it otherwise, the term "object" comprises (1) individuals, (2) general objects, and (3) categorial objects (Meinong calls them "objects of a higher order"[1]), which arise through categories, or through the syntactic forms of individual objects. It must be determined whether perception necessarily involves transcendence, or whether it may be used in a broader sense, so that all conceivable objects of knowledge can be objects of perception.[2] The second

[1] Cf. A. Meinong, *Abhandlungen zur Erkenntnistheorie und Gegenstandstheorie* (Leipzig: Barth, 1913), pp. 381 ff.

[2] As has already been established, "perception" may be interpreted in a very wide sense. Cf. Hume, *Philosophical Works,* vol. I (Edinburgh: 1856), p. 93, for example: "To hate, to love, to think, to feel, to see, all this is nothing but to perceive." Since each of these modes of perception has its noematic or

view provides for the following distinctions: outer perception, inner perception, and essential perception. Outer perception is perception of "outer" objects as, e.g., this table in
so-called "objective space"; inner perception is perception
of "inner" objects as, e.g., in memory; and essential perception is perception of essences or of general objects as, e.g.,
$a + 1 = 1 + a$. This view has extended philosophical importance in making possible the universal reflective attitude of phenomenology.

In a significant paper entitled "G. E. Moore on the
Subject-matter of Psychology,"[3] Professor Dawes Hicks
speaks of the threefold distinction between knowing,
knowledge, and that which is known. Content is regarded as knowledge; it has not existential character, and
is not a *tertium quid* between the object (or physical side)
and the knowing mind (or mental side). Here we must ask
what is meant by "existential character." In a sense *all*
things and occurrences, whether so-called "mental" or
"physical," are alike in that they are existent. It is argued
in phenomenology that if one is to speak of existence at
all it is in the original and absolute sense subjective in
character, and that "objective" existence is derived from
it. The phenomenologist, having eliminated "naïve" existence, asks how we come to posit existence, and so seeks to
determine its "original" meaning. To adhere for the moment to the schematism of act–content–object, contents

---

ontological correlate, the domain of objects is a correspondingly
wide one. Cf. on this Meinong, *Über Annahmen* (Leipzig:
Barth, 1902), pp. 256 ff.: "That one cannot know without
knowing something, and more generally, that one cannot judge
nor even 'present' (*vorstellen*) without judging about something or presenting something, is self-evident, as is shown by
an elementary consideration of these experiences."

[3] Cf. *Proceedings of the Aristotelian Society*, X (1910).

would have a first form of *derived* existence, objects a second form.

The threefold distinction is at best useful as an introduction to the many problems which are concentrated at this point.[4] Russell (*Analysis of Mind*) has rejected the notion of "act" and, questioning its empirical foundation,[5] has accepted objects as regards sensations and "contents" in the sphere of memory and thought. This follows from his rejection of the "act," it being held to be obvious that there must be a content for memory in order to have something that happens *now* as opposed to the event that happened in the past. The phenomenologist undertakes to give a descriptive account of experience as a network of activities. It seems to him that "acts" not only have an empirical foundation, for experience is always in a process of change,

---

[4] Cf. E. Husserl, *Ideen,* pp. 267 ff. Husserl refers to the essay by Twardowski, "Zur Lehre vom Inhalt und Gegenstand der Vorstellungen" (Wien, 1894), as calling attention to this useful schematism, but urges that such notions as "act," "content" and "object" of "presentations" must be phenomenologically clarified. His detailed investigations and sharp distinctions, as seen in his *Logical Investigations* and *Ideas,* show the cognitive situation to be very complex, as opposed to the oversimplification which is incurred by the "threefold distinction." For Husserl, "act" is a "modus" of intentionality and refers to the noetic side of consciousness.

[5] Cp. with Wundt, *Psychologische Studien,* III (1907), p. 347, "The *actus purus* of the thought experiments is no fact of observation, but simply a consequence of defective observation and false presupposition." (Referred to in F. Aveling, *On the Consciousness of the Universal,* London: Macmillan, 1912). Cp. with Meinong, *Zur Erkenntnistheorie und Gegenstandstheorie,* p. 397, on the other hand, whose view agrees with that of Husserl in this connection: "All judging is a doing . . . perceiving is also a doing. . . ."

but that reflection also shows the presence everywhere of active thought processes, syntheses, identifications, perceivings, imaginings, etc. The term "act" is not, however, to be used in an assumptive or ontological sense. It stands or falls on a descriptive basis.

Let us consider a concrete illustration of outer perception. The table before me as I write and of which I am conscious will serve our purpose. I say "table before me *of which I am conscious*," and mean thereby an external object. Those who adhere to the tradition of sensationalism will hold that the first factor in this cognitive act is a complex of sense-data. But the actual state of affairs is that I have a perception of a thing in space, and this is the event from which subsequent analysis must proceed. The point is to describe the thing just as I apprehend it. But do I perceive the table, or appearance of the table, i.e., the ways of its givenness to me? What I have is a series of aspects and perspectives as *such,* but always of the *same* thing— namely, "table." As the light varies, as my position varies from it in distance, as I move my head from side to side to gather a more complete view of the object before me, as my eye-movements determine various aspects, I am aware of a variety of modes of givenness of the table. In the spirit of Hume one might ask how one comes to speak of an identical object, if these observations be the account of what is present to me. To answer this involves a discussion of meaning, or intentional consciousness. Apart from such discussion, the "content" would not stand in the usual sharp antithesis to the "object." We do not have to do with a predicament, but with the essential structure of cognition. If one asks what is reflectively given when he perceives the table, the answer is, not sense-data, but *appearances* of the table; and this can be actually described and determined from the standpoint of reflection.

James[6] states that sensational and reproductive brain-processes combined give us the content of our perceptions. But "content" in what sense? It would seem more to the point were he to say that the one is object, the other subject of the acts of perception. This will be clearer with a more adequate quotation from the passage referred to.

Every concrete particular thing is a conflux of sensible qualities, with which we have become acquainted at various times. Some of the qualities, since they are more constant, interesting, or practically important, we regard as essential constituents of the thing. In a general way, such are tangible shape, size, mass, etc. . . . Other properties, being more fluctuating, we regard as more or less accidental or inessential. We call the former qualities the reality, the latter its appearances. So when I get as now a brown eye-picture with lines not parallel, and with angles unlike, and call it my big solid rectangular walnut library-table, that picture is not the table. It is not even like the table is for vision, when rightly seen. It is a distorted perspective view of three of the sides of what I mentally *perceive* (more or less) in its totality and undistorted shape. The back of the table, its square corners, its size, its heaviness, are features of which I am conscious when I look, almost as I am conscious of its name.

If every concrete particular material thing were, as James seems to hold, nothing but a conflux of those sensible qualities with which we have become acquainted, then it would be difficult to account for the obvious indeterminateness and incompleteness of each single aspect of a "thing"; and

[6] Cf. William James, *Principles of Psychology* (New York: Henry Holt and Company, 1890), vol. II, p. 78.

we would have to do, as he states, with "particular material things."

Can it be said that it belongs to the essence of "things" to be given in a mass or conflux of incomplete appearances? If one does not from the outset acknowledge things as objects existing apart from knowledge, i.e., as different from the objects-of-knowledge, then one must seek the essence of things in what is given in the world of perceptions. Instead of looking to "practical considerations" for the essence of an object, the phenomenologist asks, "What is the thing of perception if not what is *meant as the same* throughout a conflux of perceptions, and is it not one *essential* characteristic of a thing to be *given incompletely*, in such a fashion?" James' remark about the perception being a distorted perspective view of what one mentally perceives in its undistorted shape, refers to what has been called an "intentional object." There is the object which is meant as the same throughout the process of perception. In each successive perspective afforded us in perception, each respectively one-sided, we are always aware of the *same* table as a totality.

According to Hicks, the object may be either immediately or mediately apprehended, but in either case those features of it which are discriminated, and of which therefore there is awareness, will be at best but a fraction of the totality of features of which the object itself is composed. Two distinct statements are really asserted: on the one hand, *what* is discriminated is different from the *that* presenting itself in features; on the other hand, the "object" is composed of a totality of such features, but we are always limited in our discrimination *and awareness* to a fraction of these features. In the latter statement there is an ambiguity resulting from the apparently interchangeable connection laid down between discrimination and awareness. There can be only a limited discrimination of the features of a totality; but awareness there is *both of the part and the whole*. That is to say, an and-so-forth is always involved in discrimination, or in perception in general. The question then arises, how one is to know that only a fraction of the alleged totality is discriminated, and escape the danger of merely hypostatizing the object. In sense-perception the object is said to be immediately discriminated, and there the content will tend to become hypostatized and to usurp the place of the object. But there is no difference *in kind* between the contents in the two cases; and according to this view, the content is non-existent, as opposed to that which is known—or the object. (This can be compared with Russell, *loc. cit.*, on sensation, which is for him the analog of immediate discrimination; here he professes to be a realist, i.e., in this case there is no difference between content and object.) That the discriminated features of the object form a part of the totality of features of which the object itself is composed—it being observed that the object is nothing but such a totality—is a statement that might be drawn from sheer description. It might be urged that the difference between "immediate" and "mediate" is difficult to account for in the light of this view, inasmuch as it belongs to the essence of the object to be immediate (object of perception) and also mediate (object as meant in thought), since but a part of the features of which it is composed is apprehended, and yet *it* is present to me. Further, from the standpoint of reflection, the incompleteness is seen completely. If I say, "I perceive the table," table is the object; that is, when I "live in the act"; but in reflection the object is no more the "table," but "I perceive the table." There is, in short, an essential alteration of the object. Whereas inadequacy marked the first case, adequacy is said to be obtained in the second, just as it is said that we can see unclearness clearly.

Hicks asserts that, both in sense-perception and in

thought, there is a perfectly legitimate contrast to be drawn between the content of an act of apprehension and the object of that act of apprehension.[7] The content of the act of apprehension he holds to be the sum of qualities actually discriminated "in and through the said act"—a sum of qualities whose being, *as a sum,* "has come about through the act of apprehension, and which will be different from the *sum* of features composing the object. . . . As content . . . of an act of apprehension the sum of qualities we are considering has no separate consciousness of which it is the content. The content is often hypostatized and treated as an object. But the content is not rightly treated as an object." The "act," however, is omitted in the discussion. If we in our acts of consciousness perceive different sets of appearances continually, it follows that any particular set *qua* set occupies the cognitive stage only as so specializing an act. Thus the content is really the "way" in which the "object" is known. But how about the "object"? And how much more than "way" is the content, if "the thing does not exist independently of its qualities, properties, and relations"? He argues that that *of* which we are aware is not the content; what we are aware *of* is the real object, the content being rather the way in which there is awareness of the object, the way in which the object is known.

The term "quality" has been used, and is not unique in meaning. One can speak of the quality "red" as the property of the object, as its "being-colored." Or of the quality "red" as a sense-quality, and so red as a factor in an aspect of the object, as qualifying the aspect, which is an immanent object, in the reflecting apprehension of the aspect

[7] Cf. also Hicks' later paper in the *Proceedings of the Sixth International Congress of Philosophy* (New York: Longmans, Green and Co., 1927), in which he states that this contrast must arise (p. 229).

object. We can say, first, that in the thematic apprehension
of the object (e.g., red house), in the perception of it as a
house, we apprehend (among other elements) its color as
its property; second, in the thematic apprehension of the
aspect, disregarding the fact that it is an aspect of the
house, we apprehend the "colorness" of the aspect. The
first remains identical in the continuous change of the perception and its aspects (so long as we see the red house in
its redness), while the second, in the continuous change of
aspects, is different from aspect to aspect. This is the case
for all qualitative properties. What holds for the thing-
qualities, or for the qualities of aspects as immanent objects, holds also for the relations and for the connections.

Various views of the object and content of the act are
possible. To regard the "act" as fundamental is to be in line
with empirical evidence, for that is what we actually see
when we observe the processes of thought from the standpoint of reflection. An element of striving goes through
cognition; and wishing, willing, judging, etc., are forms of
act. The most universal characteristic of pure consciousness (i.e., consciousness without reference to the external
world as existent, but merely as a *cogitatum*) is *intention*,
intention that strives for fulfillment. Self-transcendence is
thus essential to consciousness as such.

The first view of object and content of the act may be
characterized as follows:

(1) I am conscious of an object; and by "object" is
meant that of which I am conscious in a given life-pulse
or experience, in a particular consciousness, e.g., this perceiving, this remembering, this expecting, this fantasying,
etc.—that is, as that identical something which is meant so
and merely so, that which is valid for me as being real, or
unreal, as being certainly, or only probably being, as
doubtfully being, etc., or a mere phantasma, as if it were
certainly there, or probably, or unreal appearance, etc.

Now, suppose we disregard the question whether the object is in truth, and is "in itself," in some sense of "in itself." Any occasional act has its object, or as it may be several objects which could be distinguished and, as always, connected through meaning. Experiencing this act, carrying it out, the "I" of the act means that and that, and the meant object is valid for it as being real, as not being, as being bodily present, as represented, etc. This intentional object of the act determines at the same time a first notion of "content." Namely, if one presupposes a world of things existing by itself, or in general a truly existent world of objects, and then thinks that a subject could mean those objects falsely, according to being or determinate being, then separation is incurred between that which the subject might mean in one of his acts and those object-qualities which are meant. The subject has consciousness of the same object, now apprehending these, now those determinations, perhaps directly perceiving them, or perhaps having the consciousness to assign determinations to the object now which it denies of it later, which it must abandon, etc.

A second view is as follows:

(2) As opposed to the identical intentional object, to the identical "this-here," the "content of this act" can be called the complex of the occasional and changing determinations "meant to" or ascribed to the object through consciousness.

(3) As opposed to the thing which might be presupposed as being truly, one can understand by "content of an act" the collective sum of all the factors that can be discriminated in it, all that the act is and has in itself.

(4) There are particular notions of "content." One could mean by "perceptual contents" (general intuitive contents) the perceived object from the occasional side it happens to be in; but then also the perceived object in the "how"

of its perceptual presentation; but also the object in the "how" of its object-determinations in general, as how they are meant in this act, etc.

The phenomenological treatment of "content" occupies an important place. Let us take as an example perception of a flower. The flower has a whole complex of properties which, abstracted from their facticity, go to make up the "content." This includes the "what" and the "how" of experience. The "content" may be vague, as in the case of sensuous presentations; one can say, for example, red of this kind, but there are no unique determinations. Furthermore, the "content" in this sense is individual, and not general. One can vary this "content," however, in various possible generalities. Instead of saying "red of this rose," one can speak of red of all roses, or red in general, color in general, and finally visual quality in general. It is thus an eidetic or essential law that in all content-components the content itself is the basis for possible generic determinations. Through a process of generalization one can come to the highest genus, or nature. The highest genus would be "extended thing," the thing of ontology. It is a further step in the phenomenological method to "reduce" everything to pure experience, and so to view the acts through which the objects are given.

B. The Object of Intentional Experience

Let us turn once more to the problem of the object perceived. Suppose that you perceive a tree. Although your total perception is made up of a process of single views, you regard the tree as the same unchanged tree. You establish its identity, purely by seeing, although it is given in aspects, perspectives, and perceptual forms. The consciousness of one and the same object goes through the continual change of perception. Your *thematic* view was, to begin with, directed to the tree; but if you reflect, it is directed to the manner in which this tree is presented to you, to the perspectives, modes of appearance, etc. In ordinary life, one mode of appearance is singled out as the "normal" one, as the necessary thematic point of departure, in order to be able to pass to other modes. This process of perceptual experience has a unity, and every cross-section of it is a perception of the tree. That which you mean (and which is meant throughout all the appearances) is the same in every appearance of the stream of perception, in every phase or stretch; it is given as the same, and you can see it as such. There is a seeing perception, a hearing perception, a tactual perception, and also a spiritual perception; you can, so to speak, spiritually put your finger on the appearance. In spiritual reflection you can apprehend or grasp the appearance itself, just as it lives. Perception exemplifies a process of *synthesis:* the appearances are connected, and they bring "the same" to appearance, which we can directly apprehend as such. Husserl speaks of the "sameness" in the objective sense. Perception carries in itself an identical sense, the perceived object. In this case, object is called "sense." The identical, same tree, or table, etc., is the first factor of the cognitive situation. The "sense" is the name for a "pole" (sense-pole) of a manifold of experiences; it is the carrier of a set of factors which can be distinguished. This analysis of perception can be made, *mutatis mutandis,* in the case of every intentional experience. There can furthermore be a synthesis in the following manner: I remember that I perceived this table yesterday; and, reflectively, I can see two consciousnesses of the same, which are united in a synthesis. The analysis can easily be extended to cover the more complicated cases.

To speak of an intentional object is not the same as to speak of a "real thing." The tree of "real nature" does not require a consideration of whether one properly perceives it or not, if one speaks of its sense. A perception is in itself perception of this tree, this table, etc. The perceived cannot be separated from the perception so long as it is what it is. Perception is, in short, an intentional experience, and has (immanent in itself) an intentional object. It has this "object as meant." We say that the tree in the picture "is" not in reality. Nevertheless there is the tree before our eyes, with its sense. There is obviously a shifting of meaning. This illustrates the significance of the distinction between the tree sheerly and the "tree" in quotation marks. The latter is the intentional pole of the perception in question. This is a sense-pole, and there is much to be discriminated in it.

The modalities of belief and of judgment can be distinguished on the side of the ego, or the subject of thematic interest; and the modalities of being are on the side of the intentional object. All modalities agree in that they make an affirmation, or refer to one. We may have illusions and not know it, in which case they do not have the character of illusions for us. They are only illusions for us when they are unveiled; and then they have the character of nullity. For example, one might be in doubt whether the object before him be an artificial model or a man. Suppose that one were to decide, after doubt, that it is a man. Then comes the unveiling and the distinction between the character of reality and the character of illusion, of nullity. The ego negates, rejects, draws a blue line through the given. The same intentional object remains; it can be the same in the phenomenon, and can have the same aspects. On the one hand, there is the existent reality (in the modus of certainty); and on the other, there is the non-existent, or null. All modalizing points back to a primal modus, which is itself no modus, but sheer existential belief: being itself is there. Non-being is thus said to contain being within itself. If a blue line is drawn through it, it is still there as "crossed-out." Every object has an existential modus. Before the decision (in our example given above), there were two objects: artificial model and man. One passes through the modalities of doubt, questioning, etc., and in each case there is the correlative being. This presents us with a series of transformations of the primal character. Doubt, for example, is directed against a being. Nothing comes into consciousness accidentally; everything has a meaning. He who doubts wavers between two inclinations. Generally speaking, the same intentional pole, or the same object, goes through all the modalities involved.

C. The Ideal World of Intention

The natural and naïve external view which places in opposition the knowing person and the known world nevertheless has its rights; it has the right to say, there is a man—that one there, or I myself—he has such and such perceptions, memories, thoughts, opinions of all kinds, and they belong to his mind; and those known objects, external to man, are what they are by themselves, whether he knows them or not. But, Husserl maintains, the last right of this schematism, or rather of these self-objective facts of cognition of men referred to the world common to them, must itself again be sought on "absolute" ground. For the naturalist, cognition as a fact of the world is itself just a kind of objective and true being. But for the phenomenologist it has its meaning and right by the grace of cognition, viewed "transcendentally." That which cannot be doubted is pure consciousness, which comprises a stream of *cogitationes*, with their *cogitata*. A presuppositionless beginning is supposedly made if one takes pure consciousness, or pure reflection, for the starting point. The title "*Ego cogito*"

names this sphere, with the "*ego*" detached from its natural
setting in the world. The price of what is called an "adequate" beginning for philosophy is detachment from natural existence.

Adequacy in this sense marks the beginning of transcendental philosophy. But inadequacy belongs essentially
to perception and to experience of the world as such. An
external perception of a thing in space is a mixture of self-
givenness, or what is apprehended, and meaning-with, or
beyondness, or anticipation. A perception without such inadequacy would be unthinkable. There is also the possibility that perceptions would be other than what they
happened to be, and even that they *were not*. Every perception can deceive one, although perception is, according
to its meaning, direct apprehension. Experience deceives,
and verifies itself through itself; and every verification is
presumptive. If you take collective perception, and regard
it as being that in which all perceptions are embedded as
moments of it, you have the notion of a continuous consciousness of a unified world persisting in infinite time, and
extended in infinite space. All this lies in *what is perceived*
in the unity of universal perception. In all self-givenness
there is the moment of anticipation, the eternal open possibility of being-different, and even of not-being. To consider this more closely: A continuous stream of external
perception flows factually, with the form of consistent correction; it can always be substituted, or does this by itself,
in the continuous process of perception. What is not verified is substituted by a modified formation, until another
break in the harmony occurs. Any perception, as a single
factor of the collective perception spoken of, will, if it is
a deception, be suspended, and with that goes a change of
meaning, a change of the perception-sense. For example,
in a fog one might perceive the shape of a tree stump,
which perception is corrected from another perspective to

be that of an animal. So doubt might enter, more or less disharmony in the perceptual process, etc. A perceptual belief expresses a simple "it is there."

The idea of a true world grows, a world that is finally harmonious, derived from an experience that does not need any correction. Natural science is determined by the idea of a finally true world. Through corrections, it approximates relative truth. It is not conceivable that the true world, regarded an idea, could ever be adequately perceived. But it is an *ideal;* and so long as the process goes on, it is necessary to posit it. It is, so to speak, a pole intuited out of the experiential process. The really perceived world is a world of appearance, given in accordance with perception. The world as appearance carries within itself the true world. In the change of correction there lies perpetually an approximation-ideal that can be approached, but can in principle never be reached, so far as facts are concerned. The process is always open; there are always new corrections.

D. The Thing of Nature

The lowest stratum of objects is for Husserl the material thing,[8] which may also be an object of use. The thing of nature is determined through a kind of subtractive process, and is what remains after one takes away other factors. A thing usually has such other layers, the deposits of the history of man. For example, a stone can either be apprehended as such or as related to primitive man, e.g., as a tool. Its significance is then due to its status as a historical object. Man comes into a world abounding in such significant predicates. It is therefore difficult (and requires a

[8] Cf. *Ideen,* pp. 70 ff.

process of subtraction, or "*Abhäutung*") to get back to the material thing. The view that there is a core in things called the "natural thing" underlying the layers of significance was declared by some to be a trace of naturalism, and merely a hypothesis. Can a thing be analyzed into a natural layer plus a layer of significance if its peculiar existential character is held to consist in its significance? It is not a subtractive process, in this critical view, but more like a "degeneration," with the natural thing a degeneration of the significant thing, and merely a limiting case. Methodological considerations led Husserl to abstract from such higher significant predicates and so obtain the concept of nature. With nature as the under layer, he had the basis for the "constitution" of the higher layers (including the domains of the various "spiritual" or cultural sciences).

E. The Description of Perception

The description of perception is a very extended undertaking, and cuts into what is ordinarily considered to be the domain of pure psychology [9] and epistemology (including the "theory of objects"). It will be of interest here to follow Husserl in his phenomenological description of perception.

Husserl makes use of the notion "phantom" as a pure mode of appearance, in accordance with perception. For example, there are phantoms in a stereoscope, with no question whether a physical thing is there. Phantoms are presupposed on higher levels of objectivity. They are in a sense momentary conditions of physical properties, or that which is qualitatively fulfilled by the perceptual sense in

[9] Although phenomenology as an "Idea-science" is no more psychology than geometry is natural science, as Husserl states it.

particular moments. We have such an object as a phantom
in changing orientations. A thing appears in the first place
as a phantom, which in turn appears in a process of change.
The sense-thing with its changing orientations presents us
with infinitely many modes of appearance. The thing can
appear in changing aspects. What must be noticed in the
first place is that an aspect is something in which a perceptual object, as a spatial object, unresistingly appears. A
perceptual object is necessarily an object in a definite mode
of appearance. If we regard the entire continuous thing
in its aspects, we see that it now receives this aspect, and
again is changed. We note which phase we single out; but
we always have an aspect, in which the object presents
itself. The object is given one-sidedly in every aspect. If
we take a continuum of aspects, we have the object persisting in a definite (albeit one-sided) configuration. Due
to our eye-movements we experience the object-sense in a
multiplicity of aspects, but always with a one-sided view.
The question here does not concern a mere factual occurrence, but perception as such, or as varied in free ideality.
In the perception of spatial objects, there is a perceived
and an unperceived side. Whatever the aspect itself may
be, we really see only the front side. An all-sided perception is unthinkable. *Perception wants more than it can
grasp qua perception.*

Although perception is "original" consciousness, in the
case of spatial things there is the momentary aspect, the
factor of "perspective shading" (*Abschattung*). In our observation of the color of a visual sense-thing, the surface
is "deshadowed" (*schattet sich ab*). So we have a real
presentation and a co-presentation. The perceptual side of
an object is seen as a mere side, and not as a thing itself;
it is merely an intuitive core which, however, points beyond itself. How does this enter into perception? By means
of an intention which has its core in the occasional aspects
of the object, but which adds an open horizon to percep-

tion. An empty "indication" appears; the "more" is co-meant. This must be investigated further. We have the aspect, which happens to be actual, and from that point out a horizon which we see to be a multiple continuum of possible perceptions. The possible perceptions are not however actually there for us as reals. They are not given as reproductions, they are given as "indications," as empty intentions. This is fulfilled for us in acts through which we actually perceive further; and this actual perceiving further, which occurs when we attend to an object, amounts to following up the object in a series of perceptions. This is really mapped out for us by the meaning of perception itself. Our interest is awakened even by a thing affecting us from the "background." While we have the aspect, we have a consciousness that reaches out, and this consciousness seems to call out from the object, "Come nearer, turn your head!" All this lies in the intentionality of perception; obeying it, we really turn our heads, and go through the manifold of aspects which maintain the unity of the object. It is seen that the object displays itself from ever new sides. We attend to the color; and we at once have color in a definite mode of givenness. Our analysis of "sense" tells us that the unseen side of the object is not really empty, but that it is an emptiness which to a certain extent demands a content. In the striving process of perception we have awakened intentions, or tendencies to fulfillment. Every new aspect fulfills the striving; the empty horizon gains a kind of content.

F. The Object of Reflection and the Polarity of Objects

We should now ask, what is the extent and nature of the alteration of the object and the mind in the process of reflection? Viewed empirically, both the ego and the object are variables. But there is a tendency to polarity. An appearance is an appearance "of" the object; and any set of appearances is "of" the object, which as a transcendent entity is no more than a pole, a point of convergence but, so far as other determination goes, an X (to put it metaphorically). Thus, in the example of the table on p. 116, we can speak of a shape-pole, a color-pole, etc., and these refer to a table-pole. On the ego side, one can descriptively see that the successive acts of perception refer back to an ego, which is also a sort of pole. If this is a true account, then one must, in reflection, have another kind of ego, the "higher" ego, as distinguished from the "lower" ego. What has been called "incompleteness" can be seen as such in reflection.

It will be pertinent to consider the polarity of objects further. The principle of the intentional object is basic in this view. Husserl tells what he means by it once more in his *Ideas*,[10] this time with reference to the X mentioned above. The thought or believed object is to be described just as it is thought or believed. Formal-ontological expressions are used here (all in quotation marks, as the noematically modified sense), such as "object," "modification," etc.; material-ontological expressions such as "thing," "figure," "cause,"; material determinations such as "raw," "hard," "colored." Such expressions as "according to perception," "according to memory," "clearly given," etc., belong to another dimension of descriptions—not to the objectively known, but to *how* an object is known. The same holds for value-objects. It has been pointed out that every noema has its "content." Every consciousness has its *what* and its reference to "its" object. The totality of the formal or material, of the materially determined or "undetermined"

[10] Cf. *Ideen*, pp. 269 ff.

predicates in their modified significance (with the phe-nomenological attitude), determines the *content* of the object-core of the noema. But these predicates are of "something," and this "something" also enters in as the central point of unity. It is the point of connection or the "bearer" of the predicates, but not in the sense of a com-plex. As has been pointed out, the intentional object is always known in the continuous and synthetic process of conscious experience, but it always *gives* itself differently. It is the *same*, but appears with different predicates, or is given with another content. "It" remains unchanged and identical, and merely displays itself from different sides. The identical intentional "object" is distinguished from the changing "predicates." The central noematic factor is the *object*, the identity, the "determinable subject of its pos-sible predicates," the pure X in abstraction from all predi-cates, or from the predicate-noemas. There is on the one hand the sheer object, and on the other hand the *object in the "how" of its determinations.*

This account of the perceptual object will now be re-viewed by outlining the major factors and distinctions:

The Polarity of the Object Table

1. The table as a whole is given in aspects.
2. The factors of the table, such as color, shape, touch, etc., are also given in aspects.
3. The aspects and appearances *qua* ap-pearances all refer to their "poles," and the factor-poles refer to the table-pole.

Thus:

Color-aspects, Ca′, Ca″, Ca‴, . . . C-pole . . .
Shape-aspects, Sa′, Sa″, Sa‴, . . . S-pole . . . Table-pole
Touch-aspects, Ta′, Ta″, Ta‴, . . . T-pole . . .

Another tabular view of perception will supplement the fore-going outline:

Eye-movements Head-movements Light-variations, etc.	Consciousness of the *same* table persists throughout the conflux.
These determine different *aspects*. Each aspect in each factor is *of the table*. This holds for appearances generally.	Consciousness displays a synthesis of identification. Appearances are always of the same object.

It is essential to the intentional object that it be given noetically in aspects. In the diagram below, the intentional object will be referred to as Oi, the object as given in a definite manner as Og, and the factors of shape, color, etc., as $Fs, Fc,$ etc.

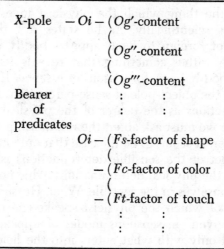

This may be represented diagrammatically as opening out like a fan, since each factor has its indefinite number of modes of givenness which converge toward the factor-pole; and the factor-poles converge toward the object-pole. Even if one had the *complete* content, for example, if a Deity had it, there would still be the intentional object, and that in essence. In Husserl's view, it cannot be conceived to be otherwise. That this conception accords with experience is further seen in the fact that if nature is posited, and if you admit the possibility of perceiving falsely, then you must make provision for *what* is the object of your perception.[11]

G. The Physical Thing and the Thing of Perception

The relationship of the physical thing to the thing of perception is of decisive importance in determining the reaches of phenomenological analysis. It is Husserl's thesis that the perceived thing itself, always and on principle, is precisely the thing which the physicist investigates and determines scientifically. As he states it,[12] the physical thing is not foreign to what appears bodily in sensuous form. It is rather something that reveals itself only in sensuous-bodily form, for reasons of essence. If one speaks of an X as the object-pole of sense-perception, and of an X which functions as the bearer of the physical determinations, then we must ask about the relationship of the Xs to one another. It seems to be the case that only insofar as the X is subject of the sensible determinations is it also the subject of the physical determinations, which on their side *reveal* themselves *in* the sensible. When Husserl states that the thing of which the physicist speaks can on principle only be "given" in sensuous modes of appearance, he is concerned only with what enters into the field of experi-

---

[11] Cf. Oliver Hazay, *Die Struktur des logischen Gegenstandes* (Berlin: Reuther and Reichard, 1915). The present view takes account of what he calls "quasi-subjective objects." Cf. pp. 15 ff.

[12] Cf. *Ideen*, pp. 98 ff.

ence. The physicist is concerned with the identical element in those modes of appearance; that is what is subjected to causal analysis. The thing which is observed, seen and handled, is precisely the thing which becomes the subject of physical predicates, such as weight, mass, and temperature. It is also true that the perceived processes themselves are determined by force, acceleration, atoms, etc. The sensuous thing, with its shape, color, and other qualities, is not a sign for something else, but is rather in a sense a sign for itself. What reveals itself is, in principle, transcendent. But even the higher transcendence of the physical thing does not signify a "reaching out beyond the world for consciousness." There is, in short, no justification for an "unknown world of realities," construed as "things in themselves." If the realm of physics is regarded as "an intentional correlate of a higher order," as a further determination of nature as it appears in experience, as Husserl argues, there is no basis for inferring a world of "things in themselves," even as a hypothetical foundation for the explanation of appearances. That would merely be the misuse of a matter of "rational insight." As a pure phenomenologist, Husserl is compelled to restrict himself to what is given in experience, and to further determinations of that process. Another methodological procedure, providing the alternative of independent existence, must be considered, if a satisfactory ontology is to be achieved. But that is a theme for a further volume.

VII

The Reaction to Phenomenology

A. The Critics of Phenomenology

It is a curious fact that many reputable scholars failed to understand phenomenology at any stage of its development. This was the case all the way from its first formulation as a descriptive psychology and theory of knowledge to its final stage of transcendental phenomenology, with the requirement of a "reduction" to pure experience. Prominent among the critics of the early stages of phenomenology were Wundt, Palagyi, Schlick, Sigwart, and Maier; and among the many critics of the later phenomenological philosophy there were adherents of the earlier phenomenology, and numerous representatives of the other philosophical tendencies, including the Rickert philosophical group, for example, and Marx-oriented writers. Although much of the critical literature was based upon misunderstandings, some penetrating and far-reaching criticism has been advanced. In general, the critical literature has been helpful in clarifying the nature and aims of phenomenology, and at least some of the objections have been answered. In various publications through the years, the present writer has given attention to representative criticisms of phenomenology, and has advanced his own critical appraisals and constructive ideas toward a sound methodological phenomenology.

No doubt Husserl's habit of holding back from publishing contributed to the difficulty of correctly appraising his published works. But that was only a part of the problem, as shown by the fact that even the significance of his *Logical Investigations* was misconstrued. The first volume of that work attempted a critique and refutation of logical psychologism, or the view that logic is founded upon psychology, as well as a critique of relativism in general. It was nevertheless said at the time, just as it is still asserted by some today, that the second volume of that very work lapses back into psychologism. This is to miss completely the nature of the phenomenological analyses of expression, meaning, intentional experience, etc., offered in the second volume. Another more recent example is provided by an article submitted to *Philosophy and Phenomenological Research*, in which it is asserted that phenomenological analysis is "opposed" to causal analysis. And a similar judgment is expressed in an article in *Philosophy of Science* by Zilsel,[1] who compared phenomenologists to Babylonian and Indian priests, and asserted that "when St. Hildegard of Bingen declared in the twelfth century that rivers rise in the sea and flow uphill she certainly used a method of knowledge which cannot have been so different from phenomenological *Wesensschau*." In Zilsel's opinion, *Wesensschau* ("essential intuition," "seeing of essences") does not provide a method of testing the results obtained, and is intended to replace causal investigations—in his words, "to substitute the methods of causal research." A generation ago, M. Schlick expressed a similar view about *Wesensschau*. But, following Husserl's published reply, he felt compelled to delete his criticism in the second edition of his *Allgemeine Erkenntnislehre*. The point is that Husserl

[1] VIII (1940), 26–32. Cf. also W. Cerf's review of it in *Philosophy and Phenomenological Research*, I (1941), 513.

was merely concerned with naming the process by which general structures, or essences, are experienced. He thought that the recognition of "general seeing" or the "seeing of generalities" was an important step forward in his thinking, and a necessary step for all philosophers. *Wesensschau* is taken to mean the direct "seeing of essences." Furthermore, it is not intended that phenomenological description be a substitute for causal methods, or that it displace them, or that it oppose them in any way. Phenomenology has its own well-defined dimension of problems; and if it is successful, it should prove to be of value to all scientific thought. The clarification of the basic structures of experience and of such fundamental ideas as meaning, proposition, object, reality, evidence, etc., could not fail to have universal application.

Wundt was one of the very few scholars who recognized the significance of phenomenological analysis for psychology, even though he misinterpreted it. Thus he thought it necessary to save psychology from the errors of "logicism" and the "invasion of logic." It was indeed Husserl's aim to prepare a new approach to the treatment of psychological problems, that would signify a "reform of psychology," as Wundt stated it. But how seriously Wundt failed to understand the *Logical Investigations* was shown by his belief that it tends to transform psychology into a reflective analysis of concepts and words, which would make it an inferior part of general logic. It should be apparent to readers of that work that logical phenomena are under investigation. If one begins with the empirical-psychological point of view (*Einstellung*), he proceeds from the fact that he thinks or states "This paper is white," for example, and that he understands the words, etc. Husserl contended that it was not "scholasticism" to *look at* these phenomena in reflection. Rejecting Wundt's "*a priori*" denial of phenomenological intuition, Husserl argued that he was able to *see* phenomenological differences, especially differences of intentionality, just as well as he could see the difference of this white and that red. If one cannot see the difference between white and red, he is said to be blind; and if one cannot see differences of intentionality, then he, too, is blind, in an extended sense. Although there may be errors due to interpretation in the case of phenomenological "seeing," as Husserl points out, that is also the case for ordinary external perception. The value of description is not destroyed because of the occurrence of errors, whether in phenomenological inquiry or in ordinary perception.

In all fairness, it must be admitted that Husserl's own text at times gives rise to conflicting interpretations and even confusion. Some evidence of this has already been seen. Another example will be pertinent. Some of Husserl's mature views concerning the nature and aims of phenomenology were recorded for him by E. Fink in a reply to some critics of the Rickert "criticist" school in the *Kant-Studien* of 1933, under the title "Die phänomenologische Philosophie Edmund Husserls in der gegenwärtigen Kritik." In it he states that all critiques of phenomenology known to him missed its fundamental nature so badly that it remained untouched, despite the quotation of Husserl's words. In the course of his discussion, Fink points out that the "origin of the world" becomes a problem for the phenomenological procedure, in accordance with its requirement that nothing be assumed. The statement that the term "origin" is the eternal human question of a beginning —a question which has been answered by myth, theology, and philosophical speculation—indicates that Husserl has departed widely here from the precise meaning of "origin-analysis." The latter is essentially different from any genetic, temporalistic account of "beginnings." The distinction drawn between "dogmatic metaphysics" and the phenomenological treatment of the "origin of the world" fails to satisfy the careful reader. The basic problem of dogmatic metaphysics is said to be the question of the origin of existence, whereas phenomenology investigates the origin of the world, i.e., places in question the unity of being and the form of the world. Furthermore, the statement that phenomenology lives in the "pathos" of investigation is hardly consistent with a rigorously defined, rationalistic procedure. To what extent, if any, such passages are due to Fink, may be left as a natural question, since Husserl's name does not appear as author. The danger of the intrusion of irrational elements is apparent. They have no place in Husserl's method, although it is true that such examples are to be found in the literature of the larger phenomenological tendency. The phenomenological "reduction," if carefully controlled, will have no room for mysticism or imported metaphysical problems. But the phenomenologist must always be on his guard against a dogmatic or irrationalistic metaphysical temptation. To say that the "reduction" provides the means for "transcending the world"; that the world is retained in the "universe of absolute being," which is laid free by means of the reduction; that the world remains immanent in the absolute; and that it is discovered as "lying in the absolute" where it lay "concealed" before the reduction—to make such assertions is to recall the speculative aims of the traditional German idealism. The performance of the "reduction" does not require that one "enter into a new realm," and there should be no talk of "concealment" from the natural point of view. Expressions such as "laying free a universe of absolute being" should be avoided, in the interest of a rigorous scientific philosophy, and if all danger of an ineffable philosophy is to be avoided. Certainly a new dogmatism should not be set up to replace that earlier dogmatism which was put aside through the phenomenological *epoché*, setting all beliefs and theses (both material and formal) in abeyance. The final discussion of the "three egos" remains one of the least felicitous portions of this reply to the "criticistic critics." The three egos distinguished in connection with the procedure of the "reduction" are (a) the world-immersed ego, or I the man, (b) the transcendental ego, and (c) the *epoché*-performing "observer." This distinction concerns the degree of reflection and radicalism of approach: it is the transcendental theoretical "observer" who makes no use of any positing of the world; for that observer the world is only a phenomenon. The meaning of the distinction is clear enough, but the language is unfortunate. That it might well be exploited for non-phenomenological purposes by writers on the fringe of the phenomenological tendency is an understandable danger. The temptation to give this analysis a dramatic turn may prove stronger than the methodological ideal to which the phenomenologist is committed. The talk of "tension" belonging essentially to the performance of the "reduction," of the "tension of the egos" that determines the "pathos of phenomenology," is far removed from the rational core of Husserl's phenomenology.

Attention should be called to a recent Russian critique of phenomenology by Professor B. Bykovsky of Moscow University, published in the leading Russian philosophic journal, *Voprosy Filosofii,* in 1956, under the title "The Deobjectification of Philosophy." The question must be answered whether a withdrawal from social reality and its actual problems, via the phenomenological reduction, signifies failure to fulfill the historical function of philosophy. Participation as such in the social and natural world would not be sufficient to satisfy the Russian critic, for he would insist upon an acceptable mode of participation. But this point of criticism must be well taken, for sound, defensible participation presupposes that one refuses to be restricted by any "reduction" to pure consciousness, to begin with.

It is sufficient in reply, however, to point out (and this is the view of the present writer) that phenomenology is a specialty, a special philosophical discipline with its own peculiar methodology. One could not chide a purely formal logician for not engaging in political discussions *as a purely formal logician*. Neither may one expect an eidetic or transcendental phenomenologist to overextend his procedures. That they must be shown to have some kind of real or factual application if they are to be judged to be practically important will be granted, however.

The critical appraisal of the present writer's *Naturalism and Subjectivism* (1959) in *Voprosy Filosofii* by Professor Bykovsky in 1961 is also pertinent. The difference between that book and *The Foundation of Phenomenology* (1943) is there overdrawn. The fundamental point of view was the same in both books. It is true, however, that the program of *The Foundation of Phenomenology* was predominantly to clarify the development and nature of Husserl's thought, so that critical reactions play a secondary role. In *Naturalism and Subjectivism* the treatment of phenomenology is primarily critical, being concerned with the basic theses of naturalism. Viewed constructively, one important purpose of that book is to show the only sense in which there can be a place for the procedure of phenomenology among the logically acceptable methods of inquiry. This task of reappraisal and reformulation is carried a step further in another book, about to appear, on *Phenomenology and Existence*.[2] It is indeed possible to learn from the better examples of the literature of subjectivism; it is not necessary to repudiate them because subjectivism cannot be defended as a universal philosophy.

Mention may be made, finally, of a critical question raised by Dr. P. Naville in an essay, "Marx or Husserl,"

---

[2] New York: Harper & Row, 1967.

THE REACTION TO PHENOMENOLOGY   127

in his book, *Les Conditions de la Liberté* (1947). In France, it was important to decide whether the working class could look to Husserl for help or guidance. The answer is obvious. Phenomenology in its mature, developed form begins with the "reduction," which means with a restriction to pure conscious experiences. Husserl went so far as to declare, in his lecture on "Phenomenology and Anthropology," that the "reduction" is not a temporary, but a permanent, deliberate abstention from belief in the affairs of the world, which is to be observed permanently by the phenomenologist. What is meant, of course, is a primary condition for phenomenological inquiry, for it must first of all have access to the reflectively viewed subject matter in order to carry on "radical" or "pure" description.[3] In the place of perception and the physical or social world, there is now "noesis" and "noema," or the activity of experience and that which is experienced as such. The working class could not be expected to take any interest in the constitutive process of phenomenology. Its problems belong to the naturalistically accepted world. If, from Husserl's perspective, the workers are "naïve" because they simply take over their social world, the phenomenological procedure can only appear remote and pointless to persons who are interested in improving their economic status. And yet, if phenomenology aids in the clarification and treatment of basic theoretical problems in logic, psychology, and social science, it cannot be said to be completely irrelevent to immediate problems of everyday life. In view of what has been achieved so far, the claims should be modest. To

[3] Cf. E. Husserl, "Phänomenologie und Anthropologie," *Philosophy and Phenomenological Research*, II (1941), reprinted in an English translation by Richard G. Schmitt in R. M. Chisholm's *Realism and the Background of Phenomenology* (New York: The Free Press of Glencoe, 1960), p. 135.

answer the question that has been raised directly, however, and in a word: a science of essential relations and structures may no more be expected to show the way to existing people with their concrete problems, than a pure geometrical science may be expected to solve problems of physics. It is sufficient if something is contributed toward the solution of practical problems, in either case.

The stage of phenomenology called "transcendental egology" has been received with misgivings in many quarters. That Husserl was attempting to carry through a specialized method with self-imposed limitations has not been generally understood. One must take him at his word, and insist that he himself conform at all times to his rules of procedure. In the course of his critical discussion of subjectivism, Hicks[4] quotes Caird on the difficulty of getting into consciousness, as well as beyond consciousness. But this is a difficulty only if real psychical processes are considered. There is no difficulty if it is a *procedural* phenomenology that is involved, with devices of method suspending all questions of real existence. The former view results in solipsism, or a philosophy of psychical immanence, and faces difficulties of its own in accounting for individual and social meanings. It is easy to see that not only practices of human society—the collection of taxes, for example—but also masses of snow and ice, sharks, and leprosy can only be embarrassing to a solipsist. It is less easy to see that the solipsist's very self cannot be known as such on his premises, as Hicks has argued. For a theory that does violence to the facts about human existence might just as well pack away enough assumptive material to provide self-knowledge, an infinitely tenuous solipsistic world, and a mode of embracing all meanings—past, present, and future—to that

[4] Cf. G. D. Hicks, *Critical Realism* (London: Macmillan & Co., Ltd., 1938).

world. In contrast, the difficulty of getting into consciousness does not occur for Husserlian phenomenology, construed strictly as a method, and not at all as a theory of real psychical immanence.

B. Driesch on Philosophical Modes of Procedure

In a book on philosophical modes of procedure[5] as represented by recent German philosophers, Driesch has devoted considerable attention to adherents of phenomenology. The shortcomings of his criticism are due largely to defects in his own philosophical position. In his view, German philosophy has been in a critical and dangerous condition for some years, because the increase of philosophical interest has been accompanied by a decrease in conscientiousness, as a result of which the great achievements of the past are threatened. He traces the danger for German philosophy to three sources: first, the enormous increase in popular philosophy, especially of the so-called "cultural" and "historical" variety; second, the elements of mysticism and the "irrational" (the "subconscious," "complexes," etc.); and third, the phenomenological method—when it gets into the wrong hands. Driesch holds this to be the greatest danger, since it is the most concealed.

Driesch makes some positive suggestions of his own in addition to submitting current philosophical attempts to criticism. It is his contention that if philosophy is to lead in the realm of thought, it must set up problems and *possible* solutions. It then becomes the task of science to follow up this procedure and to decide factually upon the solutions proposed by philosophy. Philosophy and science thus

[5] Hans Driesch, *Philosophische Forschungswege: Ratschläge und Warnungen* (Leipzig: Emmanuel Reinicke, 1930).

supplement one another: the philosopher furnishes the results of his study of possibilities to investigators in fields that are still unclarified, and he receives in turn new material for his study of possibilities. Pointing out the importance of first determining the goal of philosophy, Driesch holds that all philosophy worthy of the name is in the first place the orderly apprehension of the content of experience, and that it cannot be anything else to begin with, even though it may later raise metaphysical questions. Philosophic studies of possibilities are not working hypotheses, although they may involve them. Their domain is much wider, and goes into the unknown insofar as that is "possible," i.e., is thinkable without contradiction under the circumstances. A working hypothesis may be dropped because of new evidence, but the philosopher has simply failed if a new empirical datum undermines his region of possibility. The study of possibility requires an examination of the nature of causality and of experiential data. That Driesch means to be objective in the use of his method is shown by the precept he stresses, "Be guided by the object." It follows from this that one should first determine the real nature of the objects under consideration, as, for example, in the case of heavy bodies, history, the concept of motion, knowing, inference, etc. Thus the investigation requires the determination of what is commonly called a universe of discourse. After proceeding to classification and analysis in search of the "elementary constituents," the question that arises is: How is the object related to other objects, or what is its environment? The latter may consist of purely logical, or empirically real, or metaphysical relations.

The philosopher forms a concept of a field of reality, and asks whether it is dependent upon any other concepts. Driesch construes the field of reality as a consistent system, maintaining that no proposition referring to real things may violate the fundamental principles of formal logic and arithmetic. It will be agreed by most philosophers that this is a thoroughly reasonable point of view (in fact, its denial would commit a person to a non-reasonable point of view by definition). The descriptive aspect of the world is never complete and certain, and the principles of logic and arithmetic may be founded only with the aid of a number of fundamental ideas and assumptions. Driesch touches upon a troublesome question at this point, one that concerns the nature of formal sciences: Is it possible to determine any formal description of the world of experience that will hold exclusively for it? Can this be said for geometry? Driesch believes that it can, for he regards geometry ("geo"metry) as the genuine science of space, and not as a mere relational science. He argues that the general theory of relativity as a physical theory, not as a mathematical schematic form, therewith becomes "impossible." For everything that contradicts logically intuited essences is impossible, and space is in his view essentially Euclidean. This is indicative of his philosophical standpoint as well as of his view of formal reasoning. Driesch holds that space is "intuitive," and challenges any one to see or intuit "curved" space. He holds that philosophy must here pronounce its veto and point out that space as space does not permit of "curvature" any more than $2 \times 2 = 5$. Such arguments obviously assume a narrow view of perceptual possibility. Either *actual* perception must be meant, which does not give such knowledge as syllogistic, etc.; or else perception of "essential" connections, which goes beyond the content of any amount of actual experience and rests ultimately upon special assumptions.

To a certain extent, philosophy must rest content with generalization upon the basis of the special sciences; certainly this holds true for the natural sciences. Its mode of procedure must be *regressive* with respect to the findings and concepts of the special sciences, and it can only be *progressive* in its method after taking account of them, i.e., philosophy can then begin on its own with a systematic study of the nature of reality and the conditions of knowledge. It must proceed very cautiously when suggesting a revision of any of the fundamental ideas of the sciences, and it must make sure not to confuse the explanatory with the descriptive aspects of science. Driesch is too positive in his attitude when making decisions for the special sciences. Speaking of the concept of matter he states that "something" must be there if there are to be transformations of energy, regardless of how the physicist defines that "something." The nature and role of an unspecified "something" must be clarified phenomenologically, and from the point of view of natural experience.

As was to be expected, Driesch applies his view of possibility to the issue of mechanism and vitalism. He believes that biology has made an error in scientific procedure and has retarded its progress by setting up a dogmatic and incomplete doctrine of causality. It "questioned" only within the limits of physico-chemical causality, thus predetermining its findings. Asserting that what is biologically essential is thus not found, Driesch justifies his emphasis upon the study of possibility. Speaking of the vitalistic problem, he rules out the notion of a "pre-formed material structure" as an impossibility. Protesting against the violation of logical principles which he holds to be self-evident, he presents the mechanistic argument in the form of an invalid syllogism: "All mechanical occurrences are uniquely determined, and all vital occurrences are uniquely determined, hence all vital occurrences are mechanical." That the mechanistic thesis may be stated in strict postulational terms, in which allowance is made for the organization of life and its specific behavior, thus avoiding a crude syllogistic error, is another matter. Hence the mechanistic

position itself is not disposed of therewith, and Driesch
has not indicated the only possible alternative to extreme
mechanism.

What Driesch proposes is a foundation for philosophy
using a well-defined method which is guided by the facts
and also defines the conditions under which facts can
occur. The phenomenological philosophy has pretended to
found philosophy with certainty and lay the basis for the
sciences. Maintaining that the phenomenological tendency
constitutes a danger, Driesch nevertheless admits that it
has an earnest and worthy side, although it is easy to
transgress beyond that. As a method he holds phenomenology to be misleading because it promises good results
without much effort. Everyone believes he can "see," but
few know how to direct the process properly. He considers
the categories of the "pregiven" the greatest danger on the
part of phenomenology, tending toward a neo-Romanti-
cism that is worse than the old movement, because it is
presented in language that sounds scientific. It appears to
him that the critical work from Descartes to Kant has been
done in vain for those philosophers.

Phenomenology is in Driesch's opinion a new term for
old philosophical interests, including descriptive, intro-
spective psychology, even though the phenomenologist
seeks the "essence" of perception and other kinds of experience. The usefulness of such a procedure as a preparatory stage of work for psychology (a "pre-psychology")
may be admitted while questioning the pretension implied
by the term "essence," in the sense of ultimate existential
characters of the world. It is true that individual people
differ in the particular manner in which they experience
a thing, whereas that which is "meant" by the concept
posited is the same for all. In this sense there is genuine
empirical perception, memory, etc. But, Driesch argues,
that is not *a priori*, and nothing follows from the concept

posited apart from what is laid down by its definition. It is said by phenomenologists—by Husserl, for example—that the concept of memory involves essential reference to an earlier experience of the same person. The proposition that "memory refers back," which is an example of a "law of essence" in phenomenology, would thus appear to be an analytic and entirely empty judgment. A second aspect of phenomenology, which Driesch cites with some approval, is concerned with the investigation of ultimate experienced meanings and the *a priori* connections that may be discerned in them. He calls this discipline the doctrine of the "fundamental principles of order," or "ontology" in an unmetaphysical sense. Husserl conceived this kind of phenomenology originally, and it is admittedly a rigorous science. Then he proceeded to the consideration of "kinds of acts," which led to a new stage of phenomenology. Driesch's admission that all mathematics is included in the field of these meanings may be questioned, unless it is made perfectly clear that actual experience of any kind is irrelevant to the meanings. It appears that the technique of symbolic logic had made little impression upon German philosophy, despite the fact that Husserl himself began as a mathematician and spent considerable time in his early period on studies that paralleled the Peano-Whitehead development to some extent. Finally, by phenomenology is meant the precise analysis of certain concepts with empirical reference, whether physical, psychical, or psychophysical in character. In this sense phenomenology appears as the determination of definitions of such terms, for example, as "state," "animal," "life," "force," "association," "perception," etc. These, too, are supposed to be investigated as "essences." Driesch points out the difficulties in the way of describing such empirical essences. In contradistinction to the connections of meaning of logic and mathematics, there is a provisional element in empirical knowledge, for hypotheses are set up and may be improved or changed. Phenomenology fails to solve the problem of determining that which is fundamentally essential in an empirical sense. This difficulty should not discredit it in its entirety; but its pretension to discern essences in all fields must be abandoned as groundless. Husserl, who maintained the difficult notion of essence despite much criticism, would have done better to drop the term itself even when citing its most striking and plausible examples in formal reasoning. "Possible relations" or "patterns" would be truer and less assumptive language. The extravagances to which some of his followers are led in other fields have been apparent in numerous publications.[6]

In examining the "ontological" aspect of phenomenology, Driesch emphasizes the fact that *meanings* and their connections alone are apprehended. That they appear in empirical contexts does not matter; the "now" and the "here" are eliminated. The "essences" are apprehended, and they are not to be treated as empirical reals, nor regarded as general concepts derived through abstraction from the knowledge of real things. The apprehension of essences of organic life, masculine and feminine, etc., in an *a priori*, formal sense, is denied by Driesch, the only acceptable interpretation of such essences being the determination of the possibilities that follow from the fundamental meanings. Although it may be argued that everything possible in experience could have been established *a priori* as a possibility, Driesch asserts that there is no time for a theory of the "possible" kinds of pure spirits, or for an ethics for our attitude toward ghosts and devils. For the rest, that

[6] Cf. M. Farber, "A Review of Recent Phenomenological Literature," *Journal of Philosophy*, XXVII (1930). Cf. also the present writer's surveys of phenomenology and existentialism in *Philosophie*, edited by R. Bayer, nos. 1088 and 1110 (Paris: Hermann et Cie., 1950), reprinted in chap. VIII of this book.

which is determined as a form of essence in this manner
is not yet shown to be essential to the world, which is the
point of real interest.

This is serious criticism of some aspects of the phenomenological tendency, and it appears most just and necessary
in relation to the empirical sciences. However, allowance
must be made for the treatment of pure forms as possibilities that may find an exemplification in experience. It
would be misleading to speak of such forms as *a priori*,
since they are derived through abstraction from actual oc-
casions of experience, to begin with, and their holding-
value is purely formal and relative to certain basic assumptions. Inasmuch as the historical meaning of the *a priori*
is objectionable, claiming more for scientific knowledge
than the evidence warrants, it would be better to avoid use
of the expression under any conditions. Driesch's criticism
is pertinent in pointing out the fruitless and erroneous nature of the *a priori* study of essences in the field of empirical
fact, and the error of attempting to "deduce" all particular
things from general, *a priori* concepts. The necessity of
such criticism is illustrated by the *a priori* "intuition" of
such an adherent of phenomenology as Scheler, who held
that the essence of man could be discerned, and that from
this apparent intuition it may be deduced that men must
have sense-organs. In Driesch's view, this would be justified if it were advanced as a hypothesis. On the basis of
what is known empirically one may set up suppositions
concerning a world-plan in which man has a place. Thus
on the *hypothetical* assumption that man is to play this
role in a *supposed* world-plan, he would have to be constituted just as he happens to be, which weakens the notion
of essence materially. Apodictic and *a priori* claims are
clearly baseless in this case; and it is an error to confuse
that which is learned empirically with its possibility as an
a priori matter, as Scheler seems to do.

The phenomenologists' use of the notion of "pregiven" entities is sharply questioned by Driesch. From the standpoint of possibility, our world is one of an infinite number of possible worlds. But mere *a priori* possibilities do not help much, as is seen in the case of angels or ghosts. What we know of our world is derived empirically. How, then, can we speak of something as "pregiven"? In the sense of a formal construction, only "object-in-general" could be regarded as pregiven, but that would not apply to "nature" or "empirical reality in space." As Driesch states it, an indefinite number of "categories" is pregiven: i.e., every thinkable combination of the fundamental meanings, such as order, this, such, relation, so much, because, whole, the so-called qualities, beside, then, etc.; and for that reason *nothing in particular* is pregiven.

In point of method, however, the cognitive situation can be analyzed into its formal and "material" elements, on the basis of which the general setting of an act of knowledge as involving a world of existence and human society is recognized. It is not necessary to speak of "presuppositions" when facts are involved. If pregivenness means existence independent of knowing beings, that can be established as a matter of fact. There need be no mystery connected with the pregiven. This problem was incurred by Husserl in his last period, when he was compelled to come to grips with existence on the basis of a descriptive science of pure consciousness.

It may be well, finally, to enlarge upon Driesch's leading question and ask, What is really wrong with philosophy? Before one decides on the dangers of philosophy it is pertinent to inquire about its importance in the world at large and the extent to which its utterances make a difference. It appears that Driesch has overestimated the significance of philosophical movements and tendencies for the German people as a whole. The usual ventures of philosophy touch only remotely upon the principal problems confronting human society. They may be "eliminated" as belonging to the factual realm if one follows Husserl in the use of the phenomenological method, or they may be ascribed to unclear thinking. For, it has been said, is not clear thinking prerequisite to right conduct, and are not the philosophers specialists in clear thinking? It would follow that our first task must be the achievement of unity among philosophers in order to prepare the way for just action. This ultra-rationalistic attitude has had its adherents. The strife among philosophers is proverbial. One thinks of logical, illogical, and non-logical philosophers. But even if unity among philosophers could be achieved, that would make little difference in the world at large, and certainly not to the basic problems of society. This judgment is based on the nature of most of the subjects that interest present-day philosophers, and on some of their utterances in connection with wars and social conflicts. It would seem that universal agreement among nations and internal harmony in each country are prerequisite to agreement among philosophers. That a thoroughly scientific philosophy, realized in a universal system of education, would be effective must be granted. However, such an ideal plan presupposes ideal conditions. Philosophy holds up the ideal of universal happiness, but the best that many of its exponents can offer is renunciation. Small wonder, then, that they retire to their own special problems with a specially invented terminology, differing sometimes from case to case, and in their peculiar methods. The phenomenologists desire certainty to begin with, but fail to achieve it. They would do much better to start with the ineradicable problems of experience, which should satisfy the demand for certainty. The danger incurred by "pure" philosophizing is that one may forget the primary purpose of knowledge, which is control by man over the natural environment and human relations.

Philosophers may rightly attempt to improve the real world, which is "given" and in large part "pregiven," in the sense that it cannot even be wished away; but they should not try to improve upon the real world unless they make it clear that they are resorting to fantasy.

Although quite helpless when confronted by the most important social problems, philosophy does have a certain amount of significance for science, mainly because of the development of logic. In some cases it continues to be the handmaid of theology, or, again, it attempts to make provision for religious faith. It is sufficient to mention here the attempts to construe religion in terms of moral value, and the attitude that "a person may believe as he pleases," which is restated in philosophy as the privilege to justify implicit faith in transexperiential and ultimate matters on the pragmatic ground of their agreeableness. This is one of the points at which philosophy makes explicit contact with human society. Survival plays an unusually large role in philosophy, as is illustrated by the highly eclectic nature of most systems and the persistence of the traditional tendencies, with the result that traditional "schools" tend to be perpetuated at the expense of a growing scientific philosophy. This suggests another "danger" for philosophy.

The "ultimate meanings" of both Driesch and the phenomenologists indicate the deductive ideal of philosophy. Guided by the principle of parsimony in admitting ideas as ultimate, it becomes the task of philosophy to clarify them. On the purely descriptive side, one set of postulates cannot be adequate for the foundation of philosophy and science, for special postulates must be added as the subject-matter and facts require them. Underlying all ordered knowledge there must be general principles and commitments concerning existence, including human existence. For this reason there can be no final truth or proof in a theoretical sense. The established facts of existence provide the basis for all philosophical thought. Philosophers should at least recognize candidly the essential limitations of the philosophical enterprise, limitations which we at once accept and ignore when we speak of "practice." In the significant essay which appeared in *Logos* in 1911, "Philosophy as a Rigorous Science," Husserl sketched the ideal of a thoroughly scientific philosophy, which would be justified step by step by evidence and rigorous logical procedures. Philosophy has not tended to approach that ideal to any great extent. The path of philosophy is indeed beset with dangers.

C. Cassirer on the Phenomenology of Knowledge

Professor Cassirer's work on the phenomenology of knowledge[7] is the third volume of his general treatise on the philosophy of symbolic forms; it presents a valuable summary of a large portion of recent scientific scholarship with philosophical significance. The term "phenomenology" is intended to be used in Hegel's sense rather than in any modern sense. There is a resemblance to Husserl's phenomenology, however, and considerable evidence of influence from that source. The author regards his view as being broader than that of Kant; it is not limited to scientific knowledge to begin with, but is concerned rather with all modes of understanding the world. Like Kant, he maintains the activity of mind, or "spiritual formation," and believes that the understanding furnishes the law and order to scientific experience and its objects. But the exact

[7] Ernst Cassirer, *Philosophie der symbolischen Formen,* Book III: *Phänomenologie der Erkenntnis* (Berlin: Bruno Cassirer, 1929); discussion published in *The Philosophical Review,* XLIV (1935).

scientific forms of thought are not the only ones. There are others, as illustrated in the author's studies of language and mythology, to which reference is frequently made. In the present volume he is led to ask whether the analysis of consciousness can lead to a final, original source which is incapable of further analysis, and which is known as the ultimate constituent of all reality. The old and objectionable assumption at the basis of this point of view is that everything relative must finally be based on an absolute ground, so that scientific concepts with relative validity are led back to ultimate and necessary presuppositions.

The relation of mind and body is held up as a first model for a purely symbolic relation which is not reducible to causal or thing-relationships. Connections of meaning of this kind are regarded as the constitutive presuppositions or necessary conditions for things and their relationships. The symbolic function of presentation and that of meaning first give access to an "objective" reality, and thus make possible the perception of a determinate reality. The term "objective" is placed in quotation marks characteristically enough, for the philosopher is prone to question all things natural. The world itself is first "made possible" by a meaning that can only be derived from itself. It is misleading, to say the least, to ask how a world of existence is possible. The expression "makes possible" presumably refers to necessary conditions, as indicated by Cassirer's interest in the extent to which the rich and diversified texture of the perceptual world is itself conditioned and permeated by "definite spiritual energies." The rejection of the realistic "assumption" concerning the nature and structure of the world of things shows the present phenomenological method to be inadequately concerned with experience. The element of sameness as a most important feature of experience may be accounted for as a condition of survival or of successful living; and the original fact of experience is that of taking hold of objects. Such considerations are a wholesome reminder of what should be the basis of all philosophical thinking.

Professing interest in the objectifying contribution of the pure intuition of space, Cassirer stresses the role of the fundamental theoretical function of unification which dominates all spatial relations. It is not entirely clear whether this "unity of the theoretical function" has metaphysical status or is a mere construction. If it has methodological significance only, the emphasis should be on the fact that we live in a world containing real spatial relations. It is then possible to abstract from the real world and trace out the account of knowledge or experience phenomenologically.

The treatment of time follows the same pattern as that of space. Thus we learn that it is the peculiarity of the temporal schematism that first makes possible the form of objective experience. The analysis proceeds from the ideal to the real, or from the intention to its object. It is Cassirer's curious belief that if one proceeds from the metaphysical category of substance, no way leads back to the pure intuition of time. It may be inferred that he is unaware of the dogma which underlies his reasoning. As a matter of knowledge we begin with actual experience, but this is known as being but a part of a larger field of existence and events, and it indicates that larger field. The "metaphysical" basis does not render impossible either a mathematical or a psychological theory of time. It may be suggested that nothing is lost if the "pure intuition of time" is sacrificed, unless a transcendental loss can be shown to have real meaning. The author's contention, that the only possible solution to the problem of time is to be found in a transition from the original time-structure of the ego to the time-order in which the "object of experience" is posited and given to us, is clearly not sustained. The statement that existence and the symbolic, or that which exists and that which symbolizes, could not be severed without cutting the life-nerve of the temporal and destroying it, shows how his phenomenological method restricts existence. Cassirer argues that only a consciousness that can separate the present, past, and future, and that can recognize the past in the present, is able to connect the present with the past. This separation is the radical act in his view, and it is an ultimate phenomenon which cannot be explained by any causal derivation because it must be presupposed by every causal derivation. A simple and direct answer to this argument is contained in the statement that we derive the idea of change from the fact of change, which does not require an epistemological foundation. It is important in philosophy, as it is elsewhere, to decide which questions should be raised. Cassirer devotes very little space to Husserl, whose volume on time-consciousness was published too late for him to take due notice of it, a fact that was unfortunate for his own analysis.

Perhaps the most distinctive feature of Cassirer's book is its discussion of the pathology of symbolic consciousness. The author's careful study of this field has enriched his understanding of the process and structure of knowledge, and offers much to students both of philosophy and of psychology and medical science. In the section on the pathological disturbances of practice he is careful to guard against metaphysical dogma and urges his functional view as opposed to the standpoint of substance. It is not his purpose to hypostatize a "fundamental power" or "symbolic faculty," of which speaking, perception, and the like are various expressions. What the philosophy of symbolic forms seeks is not what is common to them in being, but rather in meaning. The knowing of the world requires that one withdraw from it, and gaining the "world as idea" is the first goal of the symbolic forms.

Relations such as unity and difference are regarded as conditions of the perceptual world rather than as part of it. Thus Cassirer confuses the relationship between knowledge and reality and falsely consigns the conditions of experience to a source outside experience. The object is described as being neither outside nor inside, neither here nor there, for the relation to it is symbolic rather than real. The term "positing" is perhaps the most mysterious term in philosophy, having been dedicated to mystery by Fichte and his successors. The author shows his inheritance from this tradition when he states that we must go back to the pure conditions of the positing of a "reality" in general, instead of proceeding from any properties of given things or the image of a reality already present. Because the concept is one of these conditions, thought can be related to objects and can lay claim to objective significance.

The attempt to determine the truth-value of mathematical symbols leads the author to set up a false antithesis between an absolute reality of things and relational or symbolic knowledge. He therewith injects an "absolute" reality into his opponents' position and mistakenly assigns a constructive function to purely cognitive forms, which ought themselves to be tested by an already existing reality. The belief that no truly mathematical concept refers simply to given objects is correct in one sense, for the abstractions mediating between mathematical thought and the realm of existence are postulated formal devices or fictions. Cassirer adds that such concepts must include a principle of "synthetic creation." While maintaining the distinction between the empirical and the mathematical world, he opposes "fictionalism" and sets up the unacceptable disjunction that either all of mathematics is fictional, or all, from the highest to the lowest, has the same character of truth or validity. He objects to the division of mathematics into real and

unreal, or fictional, as a half-truth which would destroy the
unity of mathematical method. Apparently he does not recognize that the postulational method is compatible with a
plurality of systems. The actual nature of diversified mathematical knowledge may be distinguished from Cassirer's
view, according to which the unity and the closed nature
of mathematical method is based on the creative "primitive
function" to which it owes its origin. This primitive function does not rest in itself, but is active in ever new forms,
and asserts itself in this activity as one and the same, as an
indestructible totality. It remains only to point out its
origin. The "subject" to which the pure principle of mathematical construction and the realm of mathematical ob-
jectiveness are to be referred remains the "I think" of
Kant's transcendental apperception, and hence the "pure
ego" or the "ego-pole" from which Husserl originally proceeds.

A chapter on the foundations of knowledge in natural
science completes the volume. Observing that the element
of "givenness" differentiates the physical from the mathematical, the author proposes to regard the given as though
it were not foreign to thought; in fact, as though it were
posited by thought itself and begotten by means of its constructive conditions. The form of the factual manifold, in
which perception is first presented, is to be transformed
into the form of a conceptual manifold, and that in turn
is set up as a "postulate." The harmony which the scientific
concept "demands and founds" is not mere agreement, but
a synthetic act connecting opposites. The difficulty of ap-
plying mathematical concepts to nature is due, in his
opinion, to the fact that a different order-type than the one
to which they originally belong must be impressed upon the
phenomena. It may be objected, however, that mathematical concepts may refer to relations that are really in the

world as relational events. This objection should be urged in opposition to the dogma that relations are dependent upon a relating or synthetic function of the mind.

The author's attempt to justify his procedure is not reassuring. He believes that if we adopt the standpoint of the philosophy of symbolic forms, rather than that of realistic metaphysics, the change of form or transformation loses a large part of its paradoxical nature. It is the aim of this philosophy to show that all spiritual life and development can occur only in such transformations or intellectual metamorphoses. The cryptic concept of "polarity" is taken to be the real driving force of knowledge, or the principle of its motion. When the author speaks of the construction of the domain of physical objects, this direct question should be asked: What is really built up—the objects, or our knowledge of the objects? The difference is of decisive importance. It is also necessary to separate the descriptive and the explanatory or hypothetical aspects of physical knowledge. Purely explanatory physical principles do not effect any "transformation," although they may lead to new facts, or finally be either established or rejected on the basis of the facts. The conscious recognition of this elementary principle of method would render nugatory for idealistic purposes the author's notion that a rule which connects successive perceptions is never "given" immediately, but must be underlaid by thought, even though it may be purely hypothetical to begin with. The idea that form is contributed to experience is directed against the thesis of realism. In Cassirer's words, without an ideal anticipation the manifold of empirical perception could never "close itself together" into a spatial form. Thus experience of spatial things is only possible because we build certain general systems of geometry as a foundation for particular experiences. It is correct to assert that all these systems contain at first no expression about real things or about factual situations, and that they present pure possibilities or an ideal readiness for ordering the factual. It is also true that experience as such—that is, in a narrow sense—contains no principle for the generation of such possibilities, and that its role is limited to making a selection from among them for application to a given concrete case. This is not to admit, however, that thought contributes the order to the "given." On the contrary, it discovers the order, or at best anticipates it by means of its own devices.

The concession to Berkeley's point of view is not justified, viz., the supposition that so long as we remain on the ground of perceptual consciousness, there appears to be no serious hindrance in the way of a strict elaboration of the thesis esse is percipi. The fallacious use of the term "idea" vitiates this thesis, and its presuppositions are unwarranted. It is not true to perceptual experience itself, which is precisely what is in question. Cassirer adds that the object of physics passes beyond Berkeley's analysis, for every component of this object must undergo a kind of transsubstantiation before it can be used for its construction; that is, it must be transformed from a mere impression of the senses into pure values of measurement. The author goes so far as to say that the fundamental concepts of physics are genuinely synthetic concepts as Kant defined them. His "absolute" consciousness is even less in evidence than Kant's, which leaves the synthesis quite inexplicable; it "founds," but has no foundation itself.

Cassirer argues that the objectivity of physics is not shaken by abandoning "thingishness," and holds that it is founded in a new and deeper sense. In his view the problem of objectivity is not a problem of presentation; it is a pure problem of meaning. The ultimate implication of his analysis is revealed in the conclusion that what we call the object is no longer something that can be schematized or realized in perception with spatial and temporal properties, but is rather a *point of unity* to be grasped by thought. The object as such can never be "presented"; it is an *X* in the Kantian sense, "by reference to which ideas have a synthetic unity." This conclusion is a disappointing reduction to nothingness of many excellent insights and interpretations of scientific method.

D. Misch on the Philosophy of Life and Phenomenology

Professor Misch's work,[8] dedicated to Edmund Husserl, deals with the philosophies of Dilthey, Husserl, and Heidegger. The publication of Heidegger's *Sein und Zeit* led Misch to consider its significance in connection with Husserl's controversy with Dilthey concerning "Historismus und Weltanschauungslehre."

The exposition of Heidegger's thought presents the greatest difficulty. As Misch describes it, Heidegger's purpose is not to build up an "idea of existence" in the form of a system, but rather to grasp systematically life itself, or the inner moving structure of existence, out of which the interpretations proceed. The interpretation of human existence is only a "preparation" or means to answer the question concerning the "meaning of being." Thus the purpose is not a philosophy of life or philosophical anthropology, but "fundamental ontology." The general plan of a philosophical preparation for the special sciences with their various materially circumscribed regions of being is of course reminiscent of Husserl, if not a direct adoption. Only, Heidegger is careful to stress the fundamental phenomenon "I

[8] Georg Misch, *Lebensphilosophie und Phänomenologie* (Leipzig: Teubner, 1931); discussion published in *The Philosophical Review*, XLIII (1934).

am in a world" as his beginning, instead of Husserl's absolute or pure consciousness, after which attention is devoted to such features as "care" and "time."

The aim of submitting the structural whole of human existence to a systematic analysis is worthy as a program for the philosopher. But its value depends upon the selection of significant features of human existence as shown in experience, and also upon the mode of expression employed. In both respects Heidegger errs grievously, for he has succeeded in avoiding the most important problems of human existence, and the terminology he has so studiously devised has enabled him to conceal whatever insights he has attained. Such characteristic utterances as "Man is man only on the basis of the existence in him," the virtually untranslatable statement "*Im Sein des Seienden geschieht das Nichten des Nichts*," and the expression "a pre-ontological understanding of being," are typical. Heidegger finds it necessary to deduce that the world is "essentially related to existence," which he accomplishes in a teleological manner: the world is "that for the sake of which existence exists"—namely, in the state of "being lost"—out of which the drive for independence leads. Such passages may be selected as justification for the suggestion that a philosopher should either adopt a clear and logical medium of expression or else restrict himself to the ineffable. Misch's heroic effort at exposition is laudable but hardly satisfactory at this point.

Husserl's controversy with Dilthey, the opposition between philosophy conceived as a rigorous science, as first set forth by Husserl in his *Logos* essay, and philosophy as a world-view, and the section on Husserl's critique of logical reason as illustrated in his *Formale und transzendentale Logik,* are among the most valuable portions of the work from the point of view of conveying information. Dilthey formulated the methodological principle of his philosophy of life as "the aim to understand life in terms of itself." Misch rightly observes that this principle is itself historically conditioned. The philosophy of life denies the absolute beginning of philosophy, and in this respect it stands on the ground of Kant, for whom also there was no problem of a beginning. Dilthey begins with "life," but that does not mean analyzing it. It means rather that one must re-live it in its forms and inwardly draw the consequences implicit in it. Philosophy is an activity that brings life to consciousness—i.e., the subject in its relations as something vital—and thinks it through to the end. According to Husserl, Dilthey's standpoint is historical relativism, its logical consequence skepticism. Husserl's thoroughgoing difference with Dilthey is seen in his contrast of "world-view" and science. By "world-view" is meant an idea of a goal lying in the finite; whereas the idea of science is "supertemporal." Therefore there is a fixed distinction between genuine philosophy and historically directed "world-view philosophy." It is Husserl's contention that a movement of cultural science attempting to set itself up as a philosophy is beset by an inner contradiction.

That the presentation of Husserl's own attempt at a scientific construction of philosophy may be coherently set forth is a tribute to his clarity of thought, whether or not one agrees with his metaphysics. A critical comparison of these divergent philosophies calls attention strikingly to the fact of their far-reaching disagreement over the beginning, method, and even subject-matter of philosophy. Husserl conceives philosophy as a rigorous science in which every proposition is established by means of adequate insight and foundation; he protests in his *Logos* essay against the procedure of traditional philosophers in setting up finished systems like so many full-grown Minervas emerging from the Godhead of Zeus, only to be stored up in the museum of the history of philosophy. The ideal of a descriptively founded philosophy may be held up as a final definition of what we would like to achieve if we adopt the scientific ideal in philosophy.

One might find a step toward the correction of the phenomenological method in its subjective form in the work of Dilthey. The "artificial isolation" of the subject, which destroys the vital connections of empirical consciousness, may be avoided by the substitution of Dilthey's more comprehensive "principle of experience" for the "principle of consciousness."

Professor Misch's volume is useful as a portrayal of the most important movement in recent German philosophy, but it contains little criticism of a fundamental nature; this is not surprising in view of his indebtedness to and admiration for the thinkers under discussion.

E. Xirau on Love and the World

Joaquin Xirau, a professor of philosophy at the University of Barcelona, and then at the University of Mexico, was a distinguished student of Husserl's thought.[9] In his speculative book, *Amor y Mundo*,[10] he shows the influence of recent German and French philosophy. The study of phenomenological literature was so important for the formation of his views that, as he remarked elsewhere, in order to understand them it is necessary to keep in mind the problems resulting from the contact between the thought of Husserl and the criticisms deriving from vitalism and existential philosophy.

[9] J. Xirau, *La Filosofía de Husserl* (Buenos Aires: Editorial Losada, 1941).

[10] El Colegio de Mexico, 1940; discussion published in *Philosophic Abstracts* (1945).

In *Amor y Mundo,* which the author considered to be merely a stage in the construction of an independent philosophy, a clue to the nature of the world is provided by the concept of "love." The life of our spirit is regarded as unfolding itself in a circuit of love. Philosophy and, indeed, all culture are viewed as having their deepest root and their final culmination in the desire of the loving life. Xirau provides a background for his conception by reference to classical antiquity and the Christian movement. He undertakes to determine the essence of the consciousness of love in relation to the life in which it exists (and this life always has a "logos" implicitly present) and to the world which it illuminates. In other words, it endeavors to illustrate the function of the activity of love in perception, the consciousness and valuation of individuals, and the things that surround us, in the organization of the world in which we live, and in the orientation of reality and life. Although the complete investigation would lead to ontology, the author refrains from metaphysical questions, his purpose being a preliminary descriptive study as a basis for further work.

Prominent in Xirau's work is an extended criticism of science, which is not, however, intended to be antiscientific. He is emphatic in urging the inadequacy of "materialistic science"; and the conception of truth as utility is judged to be a subterfuge. He declares that reason may not be renounced by a rational being, and that science is, throughout, an employment of reason. There is no necessity to choose between science and life, in his view; there is no dilemma. The desired middle road would recognize all the rights of science without destroying the "illusions" of life. The error of one-sidedness is ascribed to a false interpretation of the results of the sciences. Thus the claim of suppressing all metaphysics may be made while surreptitiously converting science into a new metaphysics. If the entire universe is reduced to elements such as atoms, "blind impulses," etc., the author asks, how is the appearance of this very science to be explained? For science is construed as intelligence, order, reason. Denying that the meaning of life may be explained by scientific equations, Xirau declares that it is not possible to imagine consciousness as dependent on extension; and he questions the possibility of conceiving a system of truths, and the very distinction between truth and error, in a world subject solely to causal determinism.

Some of Xirau's arguments have a familiar ring to philosophical readers. Thus consciousness cannot be explained by science because science is a phenomenon of consciousness. In other words, all phenomena are found in consciousness, and the latter does not admit of explanation. As he sees it, to explain something is to say what it is when it does not appear, before and after its manifestations. But consciousness is "pure presence." In addition, only that which is not clear can be explained, whereas consciousness, immediate experience, is by definition the evident, the clear. Objecting to "the reduction of the whole world to natural reality," Xirau contends that the scheme of science cannot explain the totality of experience and life. The mathematical construction contributed by physics only has sense in reference to a chromatic and pluriform reality, and the author maintains that concrete and living experience, with all its finite perspectives, should not be sacrificed to one of these, even though it be one of the most fundamental. Because consciousness, justice, and love are not "things," nature cannot be the whole of reality.

The positive outcome of the discussion is indicated in the discussion of "Love and the Hierarchy of Values." Love is regarded not only as the supreme value, but as the origin or necessary condition of all value. It turns out that all love is good, and that the goodness of love consists in the love itself. There is no imperative outside love, the only imperative being to love everything and to seek value in everything. The non-existence of evil results from this principle.

Great care must be taken in criticizing science and its philosophical generalization, even in the interest of a more inclusive view, if hostility to science is not to be suggested. The concept of science may be construed so widely that no organized knowledge falls outside its scope. Thus there is a *science of value,* or rather, a number of sciences converge and cooperate for the purposes of a general theory of value. Indeed, philosophy in general should be conceived as a science, at least ideally. The argument concerning the incompleteness of science is met thereby. If no region, or set of concepts, is to be left obscure—with negative results at best, based upon temporary limits of scientific analysis at a given time—the general philosophical program should provide for the ordering of everything in the universal system of science.

As for the problem raised by Xirau of an independent, identical being, a being that is transcendent of experience, it is not enough to characterize this as a "rational demand." Phenomenologically, there is unavoidably a "synthesis of identification" in all cognition. To account for the concept of the world on that basis has its peculiar value, and also its limitations, a theme which is merely touched upon by Xirau. The present writer questions the broad use of the term "love," which goes so far as to nullify evil. No view which does not recognize the reality of evil can be satisfactory for purposes of life. On the contrary, it may well be dangerous in its implications, in a manner surely foreign to the author's intention. The present writer also questions the claim that anything is incapable of explanation on a "natural" basis, as well as Xirau's use of the concept of the "supernatural." It may be that the animated style of presentation and the large amount of ground covered led him to decide against the closely knit logical analysis he would have to offer in order to satisfy all readers.

F. Noack on the Reform of Science

Noack has presented investigations that are designed to contribute toward the foundation of a philosophical science of knowledge,[11] and it includes an introduction to contemporary literature on the science of knowledge. The subject is related to the needs of life and of our existence and the author is concerned to point out the unity of science, which turns out to have political significance. The selection of material on the philosophy of language is of some value to the student. Particular attention is devoted to the concepts of symbolism and existence, the latter being described as the most concentrated concept of racial-social-personal, fateful-historical factuality. In his discussion of the classification of the sciences the author rejects the bifurcation into natural and cultural sciences on the ground that the total work of every science is connected with the methods of all other sciences. It is evident that the author has read widely, but the presentation is at times burdened by too heterogeneous a collection of materials from diverse sources.

The most distinctive feature of the book is perhaps the account taken of current German political thought. It appears to Noack that there is at present a far-reaching demand for a renovation of science which is intimately connected with the recent revolutionary changes in Germany, and that the epistemological problem becomes truly

[11] Hermann Noack, *Symbol und Existenz der Wissenschaft* (Halle: Max Niemeyer, 1936); discussion published in *The Philosophical Review*, XLVII (1938).

significant in relationship to the problems of a new social order and education. This leads him to question the correctness of the opposition of scientific and "extrascientific" activity, and to settle accounts with what he terms the ideals of the new Germany; this he manages to do by means of quotations from a work by A. Rosenberg and a general reorientation of his materials. Thus he sees fit to quote Rosenberg to the effect that every race has its soul, and every soul its race, its own inner and outer architectonic, its characteristic form of appearance. This supposedly supports the author's belief that a world-view is born with a person and can only be "awakened" and strengthened or "schooled." Despite changes in a person's idea of the world, its main feature, which is identical with the law of his personality, remains the same. Hence one cannot hope to persuade anyone by means of grounds and proofs. Agreement is only to be found where there is racial and social relatedness. In the struggle for freedom in the German sense, the idea of freedom of investigation and teaching is "suspended" by the requirement of "political" responsibility to the people and the state. The special sciences are united into a whole by the endeavor to maintain and develop the German people in their natural and cultural-historical greatness. The author maintains that the neutral-objective or the non-political attitude is objectionable today because it is not compatible with the necessities of the German people, and he recognizes that it can become a danger. The suggested reform of science is held to require the education of a new academic type of human being. "Political science" and "political university" are the names used to designate the aims of the new formation.

It is unnecessary to point out the misleading use of such vague generalities as "people" and "state" in the present context. The author's renunciation of objective and detached methods of investigation amounts to the abandonment of philosophy itself. It is the antithesis of philosophy as a rigorous science, which represented the high point of German philosophy.

G. The Influence of Husserl

The international influence of Husserl was fittingly recognized by the organization of the International Phenomenological Society, founded at a meeting in New York City in 1939. The aim of the new organization was to further the understanding, development, and application of phenomenological inquiry as inaugurated by Edmund Husserl. Plans for the publication of a quarterly journal were approved. The publication of the journal, entitled *Philosophy and Phenomenological Research,* was undertaken by the University of Buffalo (now the State University of New York at Buffalo) under the editorship of the present writer, in cooperation with a distinguished group of American and foreign scholars. The name of the publication retained the title of Husserl's own *Jahrbuch für Philosophie und Phänomenologische Forschung,* which had ceased to appear after the accession to power of the Nazis. It was made clear, however, that there was to be no spirit of a "school" or "sect," and that there were to be no restrictions through feelings of loyalty or piety. The central interest of the publication was in philosophy as a descriptive discipline. This was construed broadly to include the philosophical studies of scholars who are far removed from transcendental phenomenology as a universal philosophy, but who nevertheless have much in common with its descriptive program. The journal was also from the outset hospitable to the entire field of philosophical scholarship in all countries, insofar as space permitted. In this way, it was not necessary to debate the question of the range and

varieties of description, which was still so much in need of
scholarly exploration. The general policy of encouraging
discussion with representatives of other movements was a
departure from the comparatively isolationist policy of
Husserl's *Jahrbuch*. There is good reason to suppose that
he unqualifiedly approved only his own contributions to
that publication. It was characteristic of Husserl that he
stood alone. He always endeavored to make further progress, right up to his last efforts. He could on occasion speak
scornfully of "the phenomenologists," who rarely operated
in the increasingly rarefied atmosphere of his transcendental realm. But, late in life, he looked hopefully to the
"brotherhood" of phenomenologists the world over, the
spirit of which he believed was felt by all of them.

The widespread influence of Husserl is all the more remarkable when one considers the fact that he really stood
alone. Almost no one fully understood him; and he once
remarked that it was only in Freiburg that one could really
"enter into" phenomenology. Nevertheless, he did not dis-
courage the diversified types of scholars who attached
themselves to the larger phenomenological tendency. A
number of general negative characteristics were common
to all of them: they were opposed to naturalism and materialism; they were critical of the philosophies reflected by
the special sciences; and they were opposed to Marxism.
Positively, however, there was little unanimity of opinion:
there were "realistic" and "idealistic" phenomenologists,
religious and irreligious members of the tendency, ration-
alists and fideists. Thus, although Husserl regarded Professor Pfänder of Munich as a "dogmatic metaphysician,"
the latter played a prominent part in the phenomenological
tendency. Husserl's assistant of the First World War
period, Edith Stein, became a Carmelite nun, and under
the name of Sister Benedicta a Cruce wrote books in the

Catholic tradition, in which she is held in high esteem. Although she was put to death by the Nazis, her writings have been preserved. Her book on *Finite and Eternal Being* was published posthumously in Louvain and Freiburg. Her well-known dissertation, *On the Problem of Empathy*, has recently appeared in an English translation;[12] and Professor Ingarden has published his valuable correspondence with her in *Philosophy and Phenomenological Research*.[13]

Max Scheler was, next to Husserl, the most influential of the early phenomenologists. He read widely, and reacted to some of the leading ideas in the social sciences of his generation. He was a phenomenologist among other things, and his writings show how he responded to diverse motives. Like Husserl, he was a strong foe of scientific naturalism. In his view, the idea of "absolute monogamy" can never be derived from naturalistic presuppositions; and the belief that "marriages are made in heaven" has a deeper meaning in terms of essences and essential connections. Defending the reality of such phenomena as "holy love," he maintained that they cannot be analyzed in "naturalistic" terms.

Scheler interpreted Husserl's procedure of connecting the knowledge of Ideas to a "phenomenological reduction" in the light of Plato's vision of Ideas as turning the soul away from the sensuous content of things. While not in complete agreement with Husserl's theory of the "reduction," Scheler regarded it as signifying the act which really defines the human spirit. But Scheler did not grasp the real methodological nature of the "reduction," which he inter-

[12] E. Stein, *On the Problem of Empathy*, trans. by Waltraut Stein (The Hague: Martinus Nijhoff, 1964).
[13] XXIII, no. 2.

preted in accordance with the needs of his own standpoint. A rather objectionable product resulted from his exegesis, approaching the type of misunderstanding according to which the "reduction" involves the "discarding" of reality. Thus, Scheler asked what it meant to speak of "de-realizing," or "de-actualizing," or "ideating" the world. He disagreed with Husserl's view that it meant withholding judgments of existence. As he expressed it, the reality-factor itself was suspended by way of experiment, it was annihilated, and the "fear of the mundane" was set aside. It is evident that Scheler saw something that was correct, and that he even caught a glimpse of the play of a method. But it is also evident that his antecedently accepted set of beliefs led him to talk of "annihilation" and emanicipation from the "fear of the mundane." Scheler talked of the "ascetic" act of "de-realization." Man turns out to be the living being that can be "ascetic" toward its life. Husserl's methodological terms, "putting out of play," "suspension," "accidental here-now-thus," etc., were used by Scheler. But the admonition made by the founder of modern phenomenology that one should begin with the suspension of all beliefs in the interest of a radical philosophy of knowledge and experience, "until the final grounds," was certainly not illustrated by Scheler. It will be recalled, however, that Husserl himself spoke of the "annihilation" (or "nullification") of the world within the framework of the phenomenological method. Husserl was interested in the definition of a realm of absolute consciousness as "the residuum of the nullification of the world" (*Weltvernichtung*). Such potentially misleading language should never have been used, since it could readily be put to uses that could not be condoned in the light of the rigorous precepts of phenomenology. That Husserl himself was not free from metaphysics has already been pointed out; but he did not

respond to extra-philosophical motives of the type illustrated by Scheler's "fear of the mundane." [14]

As is well known, the aura of Husserl's influence includes
the two fountainheads of contemporary existentialism,
Martin Heidegger and Karl Jaspers, as well as the leaders
of the lively French strains of existentialism, Gabriel Marcel and Jean-Paul Sartre. To a large extent, they prove
to be continuators of the idealistic reaction against a
science-oriented philosophy, and the writers influenced by
them already constitute a rapidly growing tendency in
philosophy in numerous countries. The concept of transcendence plays a conspicuous role in their thought, but
by no means does this mean a restoration of the natural
world of the sciences. If Husserl reacted against a naturalistic philosophy reflecting the sciences, he had at any rate
considerable scientific knowledge to his credit, including
mathematics, physics, and psychology. The same could not
be said of many of those influenced by him, so that their
antiscientific utterances frequently operate on a distinctly
lower level. Whatever may be said in criticism of Husserl's
attempt to achieve a universal transcendental philosophy,
it must be admitted that his ideal was always clarity and
evidence, and that he never stooped to verbal juggling or
resorted to the adulation of "mystery."

Prominent among the scholars and writers influenced
by Husserl are Roman Ingarden, Hedwig Conrad-Martius,
Jean Hering, Alexandre Koyré, Moritz Geiger, and Oskar

[14] The many-sided significance of Scheler requires full-length
treatment, and goes beyond the scope of the present book. Cf.
the symposium on Scheler's philosophy in *Philosophy and
Phenomenological Research*, II; and the present writer's *Naturalism and Subjectivism*, chap. VIII, on Scheler, and chap. IX
on Heidegger and others of interest in the phenomenological
tendency.

Becker. Among the Americans, the present writer, Dorion Cairns, V. J. McGill, and Charles Hartshorne studied with Husserl in his Freiburg period. Mention should also be made of a number of scholars and writers who have been associated with *Philosophy and Phenomenological Research*, including some with strong commitments to various conceptions of the nature and function of a descriptive philosophy of experience: Felix Kaufmann, Fritz Kaufmann, Alfred Schuetz, Aron Gurwitsch, John Wild, Herbert Spiegelberg, Walter Cerf, Maurice Natanson, Guenther Stern, C. J. Ducasse, R. W. Sellars, R. M. Chisholm, and C. A. Baylis. The extensive interest in a phenomenological approach to psychiatry goes back to the earlier publications of Jaspers and Binswanger.[15] The late Maurice Merleau-Ponty was deeply interested in Husserl's thought, along with Jean Wahl, Gaston Berger, and Paul Ricoeur. Ludwig Landgrebe and Eugen Fink as former research assistants of Husserl, Jan Patocka of Prague, and the late H. J. Pos of Amsterdam and Antonio Banfi of Milan were, along with numerous other prominent scholars, serious students of phenomenology. The work of H. L. Van Breda and his associates in Louvain has already resulted in the publication of some of Husserl's most important literary remains, and in the series of phenomenological writings known as *Phaenomenologica*. The growing list of those concerned with this type of philosophy has rendered it one of the most conspicuous tendencies in twentieth-century philosophy. It cannot be ignored; and it is a matter of real importance to understand and evaluate it, and to align it with other serious undertakings in philosophy.

[15] Cf. J. H. Van den Berg, *The Phenomenological Approach to Psychiatry* (Springfield, Illinois: Charles C. Thomas, 1955).

VIII

The Upsurge of a New Literature

A. Aspects of Phenomenology and Existentialism: From 1939 to 1945*

I. Introduction

The literature of phenomenology and existentialism was considerably inhibited by the Second World War and, before that, by the Nazi régime. Nevertheless, it proves to be surprisingly extensive, in view of the growing interest in other countries.

In the present survey, the primary reference of the term "phenomenology" will be to Husserl and his followers, and to those who derive from them. The "philosophy of existence," or "existentialism," stems from multiple sources and has a diversity of representatives and developments. Phenomenology is one of the prominent sources. Martin Heidegger, who was a close student of Husserl's, is the founder of one type of existentialism; and Jaspers, another initiator in this field, was influenced by Husserl, particularly in his earlier work. The writings of Kierkegaard are

* Supplements A and B were originally prepared by the present writer for the Unesco-sponsored project, *Philosophie,* edited by R. Bayer, nos. 1088 and 1110 (Paris: Hermann et Cie, 1950). They are reproduced here with omissions.

163

another prominent source of influence on the philosophy of existence. Adding to the difficulty of defining or delimiting the existential philosophy is the rapidly growing tendency to use the term in an extended sense, to name any so-called "philosophy of human existence," whether avowedly Christian or frankly atheistic. Thus St. Thomas has been discussed in the context of existentialism.[1]

The dissemination of the philosophical ideas of those two tendencies has been rapid, but by no means the same in both cases. Husserl's thought remains the basis of phenomenology, and it is hardly suited for popular consumption. Like the thought of Plato, it could be much admired, or deeply studied, but not as a popular thought movement, in its original form, that is. The comparatively large sale of the Spanish translation of Husserl's *Logical Investigations* is only an apparent exception, for the average intelligent reader in Latin America was not touched by it. Only an adaptation and extension by means of a popular movement could be expected to reach a great number of readers, under present conditions. In fact, the philosophy of existence has a historical parallel to the neo-Platonic and Christianizing tendencies in more than one way. Attention is directed to man's more ultimate hopes, and a theory of human existence is developed which takes account of those hopes in a manner suited to more widespread consumption.

Included in the present survey are materials of reports by scholars representing several countries, to whom acknowledgment is made. Despite his critical reservations concerning some of the developments in phenomenology,

[1] Cf. J. Maritain's article on "The Humanism of St. Thomas" in *Twentieth Century Philosophy*, edited by D. Runes (New York: Philosophical Library, 1947), p. 295. Maritain writes: "I am convinced that St. Thomas is, if we may use a word in favor today, the most *existential* of the philosophers."

the present writer is nevertheless glad to allow more or less sympathetic reporters the opportunity to characterize philosophy in their own countries. Within the unavoidable limitations of time and space, it was clearly impossible to provide a complete world-survey.

II. Germany[2]

Phenomenology in its original, Husserlian sense was hardly represented in publications in Germany after the beginning of the 1930s. Even Heidegger and his group of students disappeared from popular notice because of opposition to the dominant Nazi ideology.[3] Heidegger did not resume publishing until 1941, when he began to publish a number of smaller writings. These writings indicate the extent of his development since his publication of *Sein und Zeit* in 1927. He had already maintained that the analysis of human existence had only an ancillary function for the gaining of a new ground for philosophical inquiry. Now it appears to be clear in which direction Heidegger seeks this new approach. To achieve it, he maintains, one must examine the direction in which the entire tradition of metaphysics from Plato to Hegel and Nietzsche moved. According to Heidegger, the meaning of the fundamental question of philosophical thought—the question of being— has been obscured. To show wherein this obscurity consists is the theme of his lecture, "Platons Lehre von der Wahrheit."[4] Being is referred by Plato to the realm of

[2] With acknowledgment to Professors Ludwig Landgrebe and Otto Friedrich Bollnow.

[3] This is not to obscure the fact that Heidegger himself had joined the Nazi Party, while rector of Freiburg University.

[4] In *Geistige Überlieferung*, II. *Jahrbuch* (Berlin, 1942). Reprinted, along with the "Brief über Humanismus," in *Überlieferung und Auftrag* (Bern, 1946).

Ideas, and this sets the pattern for occidental metaphysics up to its end with Nietzsche. Philosophy faces the task of going beyond this if it is to return to its origin. The meaning of this task is clarified in the lecture, "Wom Wesen der Wahrheit,"[5] and in various articles on Hölderlin.[6] The purpose of this interpretation was to show that Hölderlin already held the ideas which led beyond the traditional metaphysics and which recognized the question of the meaning of being in its original significance.

Of the older students of Husserl, only the work of Hedwig Conrad-Martius, *Der Selbstaufbau der Natur: Entelechien und Energien*,[7] need be named. The author endeavors to examine the concepts of modern natural science and the paradoxes to which they appear to her to have been led. She attempts to show how the alternatives of mechanism and teleology, going back to the Cartesian opposition of thinking and extended substance, do not provide an adequate field for an ontology of nature.

A work by Karl-Heinz Volkmann-Schluck[8] applies Heidegger's method of historical interpretation to Plotinus. The author is also led by the principle of the "destruction" of the traditional conception of metaphysics, according to which every philosophical system must be questioned for the originality (or lack of originality) with which it raises the basic problems of being. The author breaks with the traditional interpretation of Plotinus, which took the prob-

[5] Frankfurt: Klostermann, 1943. A French translation by A. de Waelhens and W. Biemel was published in *Les Philosophes Contemporains* (Louvain: Nauwelaerts, and Paris: Vrin, 1948).

[6] Hölderlin's hymns, "Wie wenn am Feiertage" (Halle, 1941); "Andenken," in the *Hölderlin-Gedenkschrift* (Tübingen, 1943); *Erläuterungen zu Hölderlins Dichtung* (Frankfurt, 1944).

[7] Hamburg: H. Goverts Verlag, 1944).

[8] *Plotin als Interpret der Ontologie Platons* (Frankfurt: *Philos.* Abhandlungen, X, 1941).

lem of emanation as the focal point of its inquiry: Plotinus is not viewed in the light of the cosmological interests of his successors, but as influenced by the ontological problems handed down by Plato. The aim is to show how Plotinus treats the problem of change and being, unsolved by Plato; and to examine the concept of the *Nous* in its ontological meaning, rather than in its cosmological significance.

The work of Otto Bollnow, *Das Wesen der Stimmungen*,[9] may be regarded as phenomenological in an extended sense. It undertakes, in contrast to the existential-philosophical attitude, to render the positive content of joyous moods fruitful for the philosophical interpretation of man. Proceeding from there, it attempts to show how the relationship to society and to a genuine reality outside of man, as well as the knowledge of man and things in their real essence, is possible. Bollnow holds Heidegger's analyses to be purely anthropological, a point of view which is rejected by the defenders of Heidegger. Bollnow's "Existenz-philosophie"[10] is an easily understood introduction to existential philosophy, and is primarily devoted to Heidegger's work. He does not point out that Heidegger's analysis of existence is merely intended to serve as the point of departure for a new foundation of ontology. In the discussion of the problems of thought and existence, world-understanding, fear, death, time, and history, Heidegger is treated as though he shared common ground with Jaspers and Rilke, and his treatment has been criticized as failing to point out the fundamental differences.

Among the critical discussions of existential philosophy is H. Urs von Balthasar's *Apokalypse der deutschen Seele*.

[9] (Frankfurt: Verlag Klostermann, 1941).
[10] In *Systematische Philosophie*, edited by N. Hartmann (Stuttgart, 1941); also published separately.

168

THE AIMS OF PHENOMENOLOGY

The third volume, *Die Vergöttlichung des Todes*,[11] devotes
much critical attention to Heidegger and Rilke, and argues
on Christian grounds for the impossibility of the existential-
philosophical concept of transcendence.

Mention may be made, finally, of *Die menschliche
Natur*[12] by Hans Lipps, who lost his life in the Second
World War. The phenomena described by Lipps, shame,
embarrassment, and language, for example, are examined
for the being-structures revealed within them. Thus one
may say of embarrassment that it is not something "inner,"
but that one can only find himself "in" it. Such themes were
treated independently by Sartre at about the same time.

III. France and Belgium[13]

Among the authors whose principal works antedate
1939, Gabriel Marcel is especially important for the publication of two collections of articles, *Du Refus à l'Invoca-
aion*[14] and *Homo Viator*.[15] Some of these studies add to the
understanding of the author's *Journal métaphysique* and
Être et Avoir. "L'Être incarné repère central de la Reflexion
métaphysique," published in the first collection, is concerned with the explanation of the relation of the self to
the body, a relation which is the essential theme of Marcel's
philosophy. "Les Aperçus phénoménologiques sur l'Être-
en-Situation," in the same collection, deals with the same
subject from another point of view. "L'Esquisse d'une

---

[11] *Apokalypse der deutschen Seele, Studien zu einer Lehre
von den letzten Haltungen*, III, *Die Vergöttlichung des Todes*
(Salzburg and Leipzig, 1939).

[12] In *Frankfurter Wissenschaftliche Beiträge, Kulturwissen-
schaftliche Reihe*, VIII (Frankfurt, 1941).

[13] With acknowledgment to Professor A. De Waelhens.

[14] (Paris: Gallimard, 1940), *Collection Esprit*.

[15] (Paris: Aubier, 1944), *Collection Philosophie de l'Esprit*.

Phénoménologie et d'une Métaphysique de l'Espérance,"
in *Homo Viator,* brings another central theme of Marcel's
existentialism—the relation to transcendence as anchored
in our experience while at the same time going beyond it.
From the historical point of view, *Du Refus à l'Invocation*
contains an attempt by Marcel at understanding the existentialism of Jaspers. *Homo Viator* does the same, but
with more definitely critical intentions toward Sartre.

The most dynamic of all the existentialists, and perhaps
the ablest, Jean-Paul Sartre rapidly became a storm-center
of controversy, and the object of criticism emanating from
the "left" as well as the "right." In this period he published
the two books which represent his most technical and ambitious attempts in philosophy. *L'Imaginaire*[16] undertakes
a description of the structure of the intentional object of
the imagining act. The student of phenomenology will find
much of interest in this work, as well as in the more comprehensive *L'Être et le Néant,*[17] for the thought of Husserl
and Heidegger constitutes one of the important influences
on Sartre. Beginning with the distinction between the "in
itself" and the "for itself," *L'Être et le Néant* proceeds to
the phenomenological study of the being of human existence. Although still not widely read, it has already been
subjected to much criticism. Sartre derives much from
German idealism, and this influence is evident even when
he is concerned with the *cogito* of Descartes. This is seen
in Sartre's much disputed conception of human freedom
which, he holds, cannot be distinguished from the being
of the human reality. In short, there is no difference between his being and his being free. It may well be that
excessive haste in the preparation of his material is re-

[16] (Paris: Gallimard, 1940), *Collection Bibliothèque des
Idées.*

[17] (Paris: Gallimard, 1943), *Collection Bibliothèque des
Idées.*

sponsible for some lapses in rigor, as well as for the unnecessary prolixity. But more important still would have been adequate attention to the findings of the social sciences.

Because of his close association with Sartre, and also because he has undertaken serious phenomenological and existential inquiries, special interest attaches to the work of Maurice Merleau-Ponty, beginning with *La Structure du Comportement*.[18] The task this author sets for himself is to show how the findings of contemporary psychologists contradict the conception of man unconsciously presupposed in their investigations. Both the rationalism of man as pure consciousness associated with an object or body, and the behavioristic materialism which would like to do without consciousness, are held to be incompatible with facts discovered by modern psychologists. The latter only appear to him to be understandable when they are "seen" in the light of a conception that makes of man a consciousness intrinsically engaged in carnal existence.

During the years in question, no important work appeared on the subject of existentialism and ethics. A little book by Simone de Beauvoir, however, provides a glimpse of what might have been an existential ethics—*Pyrrhus et Cineas*.[19] Without being a creative work, it clearly presents the fundamental theses of the Sartrean existentialism, maintaining the dualism which proves such an essential difficulty.

Despite the protest of Albert Camus himself, his *Mythe de Sisyphe*[20] is frequently grouped with the writings of the new school of existentialism. The book presents the personal reflections of an original mind, rather than a systematized philosophy.

[18] (Paris: Presses Universitaires de France, 1942), *Collection Bibliothèque de Philosophie contemporaine*.
[19] (Paris: Gallimard, 1944), *Collection Les Essais*.
[20] (Paris: Gallimard, 1942), *Collection Les Essais*.

Before 1939, phenomenology had but few historians in France. The book of Levinas on the *Théorie de l'Intuition dans la Phénoménologie de Husserl*, and the few pages devoted by Gurvitch to Husserl, Scheler, and Heidegger in his *Tendances actuelles de la Philosophie allemande*, exhaust the bibliography in French. Two works were added to the list during the war. Gaston Berger, whose thesis entitled *Recherches sur les Conditions de la Connaissance*[21] shows the influence of phenomenology, explains in his *Cogito de Husserl*[22] the points of similarity and of difference which can exist between consciousness in Husserl's usage and in Descartes' sense.

In Belgium, the *Revue Internationale de Philosophie*[23] devoted a special number to Husserl in 1939. Some of the articles of this number have been republished in other languages, and it remains important for the history of Husserl's thought. Professor A. de Waelhens has undertaken the very difficult task in his *Philosophie de Martin Heidegger*[24] of presenting a unified exposition of this philosophy.

Translations of Kierkegaard's works continued to appear during the war, and the Kierkegaard literature was added to by P. H. Tisseau's translation of Törsten Bohlin's *Kierkegaard, the Man and his Work*.[25]

IV. Holland[26]

The assimilation of the philosophy of existence is seen in the special fields of theology (especially Protestant

[21] (Paris: Presses Universitaires de France, 1941), *Collection Bibliothèque de Philosophie contemporaine*.
[22] (Paris: Aubier, 1942), *Collection Philosophie de l'Esprit*.
[23] (Bruxelles, 1939).
[24] (Louvain: Institut supérieur de Philosophie, 1942).
[25] (Bazoges en Paredo, chez le traducteur, 1941).
[26] With acknowledgment to Professor H. Plessner.

theology), psychology, and psychiatry. But ambitious works in pure philosophy, or on the philosophy of existence, are not to be found in Holland, with the sole exception of the books of R. F. Beerling. His *Antithesen* (1935), as also his *Crisis van den mens* (1938), brought attention to this philosophy and closed the epoch of the publication of Heidegger's *Sein und Zeit* and Jaspers' *Philosophie* just before the outbreak of the war. Kierkegaard, Heidegger, Jaspers, as well as the "Lebensphilosophie" and philosophy in the nineteenth century are discussed by Beerling in his two volumes.

Among the Protestant theologians the influence of existential philosophy may be noted. In the case of van der Leeuw it is particularly the influence of Jaspers. His concept of autonomous domains of science, such that for each domain one must seek a special method in accordance with its object, affords the possibility for van der Leeuw of an encyclopedia of the sciences, with theology taking its place as the science of revelation (but not as revealed science). Theology is held to provide a perspective for this totality. *Der Mensch und die Religion*[27] is an essay on Christian anthropology. The author does not start from revelation, but rather human existence in general, and its being-in-the-world. Religion is viewed as a condition of mundane existence.

Another original book of this period is H. Plessner's *Lachen und Weinen*,[28] which is a sequel to his earlier work, *Die Stufen des Organischen und der Mensch* (1928), on problems of philosophical anthropology. These problems are continued in *Lachen und Weinen*. Laughter and weeping are regarded as specifically human vital expressions,

[27] G. van der Leeuw, *Der Mensch und die Religion* (Basel, 1941).

[28] H. Plessner, *Lachen und Weinen* (Arnhem, 1941).

which animals lack. They are held to render comprehensible the human duality which is at the same time a unity: immanence and the expression of immanence, possible only by an "ex-centric position" (*"Darüberstehen"*). Phenomenology, aided by biology, is supposed to make visible for us the characteristics of human being, without exceeding any one of the domains of life.

A book by A. F. van Dijk on Kierkegaard[29] treats of problems of thought, in comparison with Hegel, of the individual, in comparison with Nietzsche, and of love and faith for Kierkegaard, along with an introduction to his complete work.

In Protestant theology, the dissertation of M. H. Bolkestein, *Het Ik-Gij schema in de nieuwere philosophie en theologie*,[30] applies the anthropological schema of Martin Buber on the relation of "Me" and "You" to some modern authors, especially theologians. The philosophy of Gabriel Marcel has particularly interested the Catholic theologians and philosophers. In expounding it, H. Robbers[31] has remarked that this philosophy does not ascend from the particular to the general, like Thomism, which remains for him the pinnacle of philosophy.

In psychiatry, a number of articles showing the influence of existentialism have appeared, by the psychiatrists Rümke, van der Horst, and Carp;[32] but the dominant

[29] A. F. van Dijk, *Perspectieven bij Kierkegaard* (1940).

[30] M. H. Bolkestein, *Het Ik-Gij schema in de nieuwere philosophie en theologie* (diss., Groningen, 1941).

[31] H. Robbers, "De franse existentiephilosophie van Gabr. Marcel," *Bijdragen van de Ned. Jezuieten* (1941), pp. 1–27.

[32] H. C. Rümke, "Over de twijfel," *Psych. en Neurol. Bladen* (1941), pp. 547–558.

H. C. Rümke, "Persoonlijkheid en Psychotherapie," *Psych. en Neurol. Bladen* (1944), pp. 258–276.

emphasis is medical and does not assume a philosophical direction, as in the case of Binswanger. It is the being-in-the-world, the anguish, and the doubt of Heidegger and Kierkegaard, and Jaspers' "border situations," that interest them from the point of view of psychiatry.

Finally, the publications of de Waelhens in Dutch journals and in the Dutch language should be pointed out. Although he is a Belgian, his work cannot be separated from the philosophical thought of Holland.

V. Italy[33]

There was great interest in existentialism in Italy in the period 1939–1945. Existentialism appeared as a means of replacing the idealistic philosophies of Croce and Gentile which had been dominant influences for nearly forty years. In 1939, Nicola Abbagnano published *La struttura dell' esistenza*,[34] a work that may be regarded as largely giving rise to an Italian existentialism. This publication was soon followed by a second volume, entitled *Introduzione all' esistenzialismo*.[35] The publication by Ernesto Grassi of the volume, *Vom Vorrang des Logos*,[36] in which he attempted a synthesis of Heidegger's existentialism and Gentilian actualism, is also regarded as basic to Italian existentialism.

Along with these two scholars, who are regarded as the initiators of the new movement, it is necessary to include Cesare Luporini and Arthur Massolo, who also operate

L. van der Horst, "Christelijke anthropologie en Psychotherapie," *Psych. en Neurol. Bladen* (1944), pp. 356–371.

E. Carp, "Psychotherapie en wereldbeschouwing," *Psych. en Neurol. Bladen* (1944), pp. 302–331.

[33] With acknowledgment to Professor Vito A. Bellezza.

[34] (Torino: Paravia, 1939).

[35] (Milano: Bompiani, 1942).

[36] (Monaco: Beck, 1939).

within the sphere of ideas provided by Gentilian actualism
and German existentialism, particularly Heidegger's. Luporini's essay "Esistenza,"[37] and the work, *Situazione e libertà
nell' esistenza umana*[38] may be cited; and also Massolo's
"Husserl e il cartesianesimo,"[39] "Heidegger e la fondazione
di Kant,"[40] "L'esistenzialismo di Luporini,"[41] "Storicità
della metafisica,"[42] and "Esistenzialismo e borghesi-
smo."[43]

Another scholar who has shown much enthusiasm for
existentialism is Enzo Paci, who contemplates a synthesis
of Jaspersian beginnings with those of Gentile, Banfi, and
Croce. His principal works are: *Principi di una filosofia
dell' essere,*[44] *Federico Nietzche,*[45] *Pensiero, esistenza e
valore,*[46] *Il significato storico dell' esistenzialismo,*[47] and
L'esistenzialismo.[48] In addition to all this, Paci has translated Heidegger's *Was ist Metaphysik?* into Italian.[49]

Armando Carlini and Augusto Guzzo, who are strongly
interested in thematic existentialism, are dissatisfied with
the position taken by Gentilian actualism with respect to
religious transcendence, on which they place stress without
abandoning the idealistic premises, and with respect to the

[37] In the review *Argomenti*, nos. 1, 2, 5–6.
[38] (Firenze: Le Monnier, 1942); 2d ed. (Firenze: Sansoni,
1945).
[39] In *Giorn. crit. d. filos. ital.* (1939), pp. 434–452.
[40] *Giorn. crit.* (September–October, 1941).
[41] *Giorn. crit.* (1943), nos. 1–2.
[42] (Firenze: Le Monnier, 1944).
[43] In the journal *Società*, I, no. 3 (Firenze, 1945).
[44] (Modena: Guanda, 1939).
[45] (Milano: Garzanti, 1940).
[46] (Milano: Principato, 1940).
[47] In *Studi filosofici*, II, no. 2 (1941).
[48] (Padova: Cedam, 1943).
[49] (Milano: Bocca, 1942).

actualistic concept of the empirical individual. Publications by Carlini include "Il compito della filosofia oggi in Italia,"[50] "Spiritualismo e spiritualità,"[51] "Lineamenti di una conzezione realistica dello spirito umano,"[52] and *Principi metafisici del mondo storico*.[53] Guzzo's writings of this period include "Dopo la filosofia dell' esistenza: concetto e compito d'una 'filosofia prima' ",[54] "Molti significati del concetto di 'essere',"[55] *Sguardi sulla filosofia contemporanea*,[56] *La filosofia e l'esperienza e altri saggi*,[57] *La filosofia domani*,[58] and *La ricerca filosofica*.[59]

Fausto M.Bongioanni stresses religious themes, which accept some Jaspersian motifs. The following publications may be cited: "La nozione di possibilità e il destino nella filosofia d'oggi,"[60] and *Dare e avere*.[61]

The Thomist Carlo Mazzantini, who is also an interpreter of Heidegger, has published: *Filosofia perenne e personalità filosofiche*,[62] and *Il tempo*.[63] The Thomist P. Cornelio Fabro in his two volumes, *Introduzione all' esistenzialismo*[64] and *Problemi dell' esistenzialismo*,[65] and in

[50] In *Arch. di filos.*, no. 2 (1940).
[51] In *Logos*, no. 1 (1941), and in *Atti del XIV Congr. Naz. di filos.* (Milano: Bocca, 1941).
[52] (Roma: Perrella, 1942).
[53] (Urbino: Argalia, 1943).
[54] In *Arch. di filos.* no. 3 (1939).
[55] *Atti del XIV Congr. Naz. di filos.* (1941).
[56] (Roma: Perrella, 1940).
[57] (Roma: Perrella, 1942).
[58] (Milano: Bocca, 1943).
[59] (Roma: Tip. Agostiniana, 1941).
[60] *Atti del XIV Congr. Naz. di filos.* (1941).
[61] (Roma: Perrella, 1939).
[62] (Padova: Cedam, 1942).
[63] (Como: Cavalleri, 1942).
[64] (Milano: Vita e Pensiero, 1943).
[65] (Roma: A. V. E., 1945).

his "Rassegna sull' esistenzialismo italiano,"[66] defends the insertion of Kierkegaardian existentialism into the Thomist metaphysics.

The young scholar Luigi Pareyson, a student of A. Guzzo, has come to the fore as an Italian critic of existentialism. His two volumes, *La filosofia dell' esistenza e Carlo Jaspers*[67] and *Studi sull' esistenzialismo*,[68] have met with success in Italy. Pareyson interprets existentialism as "the most vigorous affirmation of contemporary personalism."

Among other writings, Luigi Stefanini published a monograph on *L'esistenzialismo di M. Heidegger*.[69] Stefanini criticizes existentialism for its irrationalism, and for its incapacity to arrive at an affirmation of transcendence. Annibale Pastore, who was one of the first Italian scholars to occupy himself with the study of existentialism, published "L'equivoco teoretico della ragione nei fondatori della filosofia dell' esistenza."[70]

Norberto Bobbio has published on phenomenology, as well as on existentialism. These include: "Husserl postumo"[71] and "La filosofia dell' esistenza in Italia."[72] Antonio Banfi has also devoted close scholarly attention to the phenomenological and existentialist tendencies. Mention may be made of his "E. Husserl,"[73] "Situazione della filosofia contemporanea,"[74] "Il problema dell' esistenza,"[75] and

[66] Piacenza, in *Divus Thomas,* nos. 5–6 (1943).

[67] (Napoli: Loffredo, 1940).

[68] (Firenze: Sansoni, 1943).

[69] (Padova: Cedam, 1944).

[70] *Memoria della R. Accad. delle scienze dell' Istit. di Bologna,* series IV, vol. III (1939–1941), and in *Arch. d'. cult. Ital.,* no. 1 (1942).

[71] *Riv. di filos.,* no. 1 (1940).

[72] *Riv. di filos.* (January–June, 1941).

[73] *Riv. di filos.,* no. 1 (1939).

[74] *Studi filosofici,* no. 1 (1940).

[75] *Studi filosofici* (April–June, 1941).

"L'esistenzialismo."[76] Sofia Vanni-Rovighi has written a book on the philosophy of Husserl.[77]

These references, while by no means exhaustive, will be sufficient to indicate the extent of the interest in, and influence of, phenomenology and existentialism in Italy.

VI. Roumania[78]

The works appearing in Roumania in the present field of interest are principally the following: (1) *Existentà si adevàr Søren Kierkegaard* (Existence and Truth: Søren Kierkegaard), by Grigore Popa, Sibiu, 1940. The existential philosophy is distinguished carefully from the philosophy of existence. The former—of a Pascal, a Kierkegaard, or a Nietzsche—is the philosophy of a lived spiritual existence; the latter—of a Jaspers or a Heidegger—only treats of existence. The work contains a description of the modes of existential philosophy, including the ideas of truth and existence in Kierkegaard. The Danish philosopher is defended against the charge of irrationalism, the point being that it is a matter of an enlargement of reason in Kierkegaard. (2) Other works not under current Western influence are: *Libertate si Existentà* (Liberty and Existence), by M. Farcasanu, Bucharest, 1942; *Finalitate Ideala a Existentei Umane* (The Ideal Finality of Human Existence), by Constantine Micu, Bucharest, 1943 (an author who considers man to be "the inauthentic being par excellence"); *Jurnal Filosofic* (Philosophical Journal), by Constantine Noica, Bucharest, 1944.

The following studies may be cited:

M. Vulcanescu "The Roumanian Dimension of Exist-

---

[76] *Studi filosofici* (April–December, 1943).

[77] *La filosofia di E. Husserl* (Milano: Vita e Pensiero, 1939).

[78] With acknowledgment to Professor C. Noica.

ence" in the collection *"Isvoare de Filosofie"* (Philosophical Sources), II (1943), 53–97.

Gr. Popa, "Existentialism" in the review *Saeculum,* I, no. 2 (1943), 58–74.

Z. Barbu, "From Dialectic to Existentialism," *Saeculum,* I, no. 3 (1943), 44–71.

V. Iancu, "The Phenomenological Analysis of Form," *Saeculum,* I, no. 4 (1943), 25–47.

P. Ionesco, "Love and Knowledge," *Saeculum,* I, no. 6 (1943), 18–38.

E. Irion, "The Idea of Existence as the Foundation of Ethics," *Ethos,* I, no. 1 (1944), 74–91.

VII. Latin America

The very considerable interest in phenomenology and existentialism on the part of Latin-American scholars is attested to by a large number of publications. The late Joaquin Xirau's book on Husserl[79] is a prominent example, by one of the best equipped scholars in the Latin-American world. In his preliminary attempt at an independent speculative philosophy, set forth in his *Amor y Mundo,*[80] Xirau appears as a critic of the philosophical claims of science, in the context of an extravagant metaphysical concept of "love," although he was later careful to deny any intention of being antiscientific in spirit.

Francisco Miro Quesada's work on phenomenology,[81]

[79] *La Filosofía de Husserl* (Buenos Aires: Editorial Losada, 1941). Formerly at the University of Barcelona, Professor Xirau lectured at the University of Mexico until his death in 1946.

[80] (El Colegio de Mexico, 1940). See chap. VII, sec. E, of this book.

[81] *Sentido del Movimiento Fenomenologica* (Lima, Peru: Sociedad Peruana de Filosofía, 1941). Cf. the review of this book in *Philosophy and Phenomenological Research,* VII, no. 3

although not sufficiently mature and satisfactory as an exposition, is another indication of the serious attention devoted to the subject.

In the opinion of Professor Risieri Frondizi (formerly of Tucuman, Argentina, and more recently of Venezuela and the University of Buenos Aires), Heidegger's existentialism appears to be the philosophical direction which is spreading with greatest rapidity and intensity in Latin America.[82] De Reyna's book on Heidegger,[83] and the zeal with which the ungrateful task of rendering Scheler's and especially Heidegger's writings in Spanish was undertaken, are indications of the widespread fascination exerted by existentialism on receptive Latin-American minds. A greater degree of independence is seen in the case of the eminent Argentinian philosopher, Professor Francisco Romero. The great amount of attention given to "philosophical anthropology" is largely due to the influence of the German literature. It is a striking fact that such easily constructed theories are so often preferred to the painstaking, objective methods of the special sciences. It will be sufficient for present purposes to cite a number of bibliographical references.

Additional Latin-American Publications

1. Universidad Nacional de la Plata, *Escritos en Honor de Descartes* (La Plata, Argentina: 1938). Professor Fran-

---

(March, 1947), by the Argentinian philosopher, Professor Raul Pierola; and also the more favorable review in *Philosophic Abstracts,* no. 8 (1941–1942).

[82] Cf. the *Handbook of Latin-American Studies* (Cambridge: Harvard University Press), to which Professor Frondizi has annually contributed a bibliography of philosophy.

[83] Alberto Wagner de Reyna, *La ontología fundamental de Heidegger* (Buenos Aires: Editorial Losada, 1939).

cisco Romero's essay on "Descartes and Husserl" is of particular interest.

2. Julio E. Moreno, *Humanidad y Espiritualidad* (Quito, Ecuador: Grupo America, 1939).

3. Adolfo Menendez Samara, *Dos Ensayos Sobre Heidegger* (Mexico: Letras de Mexico, 1939).

4. Andres Avelino, *Metafisica Categorial* (Ciudad Trujillo: Editora Montalvo, 1940).

5. José Gaos and Francisco Larroyo, *Dos Ideas de la Filosofía* (Mexico: La Casa de Espana en Mexico, 1940).

6. Julio E. Moreno, *Filosofía de la Existencia* (Quito, Ecuador: Litografia e imprenta Romero, 1940).

7. Samuel Ramos, *Hacia un Nuevo Humanismo* (La Casa de Espana en Mexico, 1940).

8. Euryalo Cannabrava, *Seis tempas do espirito moderno* (Sao Paulo, Brazil: S. E. Panorama, Ltda., 1941).

9. Alfredo Povina, *La Obra Sociologica de Max Scheler* (Argentina: Imprenta de la Universidad de Cordoba, 1941).

10. Francisco Romero, *Filosofía Contemporanea* (Buenos Aires: Editorial Losada, 1941).

11. Julio Enrique Blanco, "Tres Lecciones sobre Husserl," V–VII (Medellin, Colombia: *Universidad Catolica Bolivariana*, 1940–1941); cf. also P. Romanell's review in *Philosophy and Phenomenological Research*, IV (September, 1943).

12. José Gaos, trans., Max Scheler's *Esencia y Forma de la Simpatia* (Buenos Aires: Editorial Losada, 1943).

13. José Gaos, trans., Max Scheler's *El resentimiento en lo moral* (Argentina: Ed. Espana-Calpe, 1944).

14. Alberto Wagner de Reyna, "La Refutacion del Psicologismo por Husserl," *Revista de la Universidad Catolica del Peru*, XII, no. 1 (1944).

15. Eduardo Garcia Maynez, *Etica* (Mexico, D.F.: Universidad Nacional de Mexico, 1944).

16. Nilton Campos, "O Metodo Fenomenologico na Psi-

cologia," (Rio de Janeiro: Institute of Psychology, 1945).

17. Clarence Finlayson, *Dios y la Filosofía* (Medellin, Colombia: Universidad de Antioquia, 1945).

18. Risieri Frondizi, *El Punto de Partida del Filosofar* (Buenos Aires: Editorial Losada, 1945).

19. Francisco Romero, *Papeles para una Filosofía* (Buenos Aires: Editorial Losada, 1945).

VIII. The United States

The years 1939–1945 were eventful ones for phenomenology in the United States. After Husserl's death in 1938, a group of his former students and friends in the United States undertook the double task of publishing a volume of commemorative essays[84] and a quarterly journal.[85] The memorial essays were largely expository of selected phases of Husserl's work, but there were also some elements of criticism. It was evident from the outset that there were very few orthodox followers of Husserl even in intent, and that the differences in Husserl's own stages of development were reflected in the nature and degree of agreement with his work. No one of the writers failed to have some degree of appreciation of phenomenology, but they varied in their own views, all the way from idealism and existentialism to materialism.

The publication by the present writer of *The Foundation*

[84] *Philosophical Essays in Memory of Edmund Husserl,* edited by M. Farber (Cambridge: Harvard University Press, 1940).

[85] *Philosophy and Phenomenological Research,* published by the University of Buffalo from 1940–1961, by the University of Pennsylvania from 1961–1964, and the University of Buffalo Foundation since 1964.

of Phenomenology[86] provided an account of the origin and development of phenomenology from its "psychologistic" and logical beginnings, and also made available the main content of Husserl's *Logische Untersuchungen* in English. Also included in the work is a critical account of the later development of transcendental phenomenology, and a warning against the abuses of phenomenology as a descriptive procedure. Husserl's contributions toward the technique of a descriptive philosophy, and his positive descriptive findings, entitled him to a serious hearing in America. His work was found to have been anticipated in part by C. S. Peirce and William James, just as his subjective program had been anticipated in England by Shadworth Hodgson. In contradistinction to those followers of Husserl who endeavored to portray phenomenology as something not capable of definition in "natural" terms, and who refused to subsume its procedure under methodology in general, the need for the larger point of view of methodological pluralism was emphasized. The occurrence of problems was held up as the important fact, and methods were regarded as devices by which to solve problems. The phenomenological method is no exception, and the talk of "purity," etc., has unfortunately served to obscure that fact. This point of view, which was intended to maintain and develop the phenomenological procedure along the scientifically rigorous lines originally projected, was also expressed in the present writer's essay on phenomenology in *Twentieth Century Philosophy*.[87] In that essay, the "cross-sectional," subjective mode of essential analysis of phenomenology was contrasted with the "longitudinal" view of the ordinary naturalistic, evolutionary method, and

[86] (Cambridge: Harvard University Press, 1943).
[87] Edited by D. Runes (New York: Philosophical Library, 1943).

it was argued that each one has its proper merits, as responses to different types of problems. In rejecting Husserl's arguments for a general philosophy of idealism—the last stronghold of idealism—and in pointing out his unfortunate use of language, which had led him to confuse experience and reality at crucial points ever since his first book on the *Philosophy of Arithmetic,* the present writer did not go to the extreme and discard phenomenology altogether. That error has occurred only too often. A strictly controlled phenomenological procedure would have made impossible its exploitation in an irrationalistic way, and the alleged necessity of the new, "existential" beginning as a correction of the limitations of a subjective procedure would have been obviated. The exaggerations and abuses of phenomenology are, then, one of the causes, although by no means the deciding cause, of the rise of existentialism.

Another publication attempting to give a portrayal of Husserl's thought was E. P. Welch's *The Philosophy of Edmund Husserl.*[88] The journal, *Philosophy and Phenomenological Research,* carried articles and discussions of phenomenology in numerous issues. Special attention should be called to manuscripts of Edmund Husserl published for the first time,[89] and to a striking symposium on "The Significance of Max Scheler for Philosophy and Social Science."[90] This symposium included, besides a helpful summary of much of Scheler's work, a critical essay on "Scheler's Theory of Sympathy and Love" by V. J. McGill,

[88] (New York: Columbia University Press, 1941). Previously published but not included in this book, is the same author's *Edmund Husserl's Phenomenology* (Los Angeles: University of Southern California Press, 1939).

[89] "Notizen zur Raumkonstitution," *Philosophy and Phenomenological Research,* I (1940–1941), and "Phänomenologie und Anthropologie," II (1941–1942).

[90] II (1941–1942).

in which the writer pointed out why Scheler could be regarded as an ideological precursor of the Nazis.

The literature on existentialism was comparatively limited, the publication of the English translation of Kierkegaard's works[91] being the most noteworthy. Kierkegaard has also been the subject of a book by Lowrie.[92] Articles on Heidegger and Jaspers have appeared in philosophical journals. Paul Tillich's article on the philosophy of existence[93] endeavors to give a broad portrayal of existentialism, construing it as "the attempt to reconquer the meaning of life in 'mystical' terms after it had been lost in ecclesiastical as well as in positivistic terms." The term "mystical" is defined by Tillich as "a venture of faith toward union with the depths of life, whether made by an individual or a group." The *Partisan Review* has maintained a steady interest in the philosophy of existence, including the Jaspers tendency. Introductory articles by Cerf[94] and Werkmeister[95] were intended to contribute a first approach to Heidegger's thought, which was admittedly foreign to the American tradition and taste—and the present writer would also add, standards. The prestige of the special sciences, including the social sciences, is so great in America, and the necessity of scrupulously observing the canons of logic is so generally accepted, that broad pronouncements on the nature of man can only be received with calm and questioning detachment. In attempting to do justice to all phases of experience, one should not forget the rigorous

[91] Princeton University Press and Oxford University Press.

[92] *A Short Life of Kierkegaard* (Princeton, N.J.: Princeton University Press, 1942).

[93] *Journal of the History of Ideas*, V (1944), 44–70.

[94] "An Approach to Heidegger's Ontology," *Philosophy and Phenomenological Research*, I (1940–1941).

[95] "An Introduction to Heidegger's Existential Philosophy," *Philosophy and Phenomenological Research*, II (1941–1942).

concept of evidence of phenomenology. Unfortunately, the literature of existentialism frequently does not measure up to phenomenological requirements any more than it satisfies the demands of the special sciences. As a philosophical shortcut it may gradually come to supersede idealism as a general tendency, for idealism in America has shown little capacity for further inventiveness and adaptation. Bearing in mind the conservative and often antiscientific role played by idealism, this is a dubious distinction to assign to the new tendency.

B. Aspects of Phenomenology and Existentialism: From 1945 to 1948

The numerous publications in the field of phenomenology, and the enormous amount of material bearing on existentialism in so many countries, make a complete survey impossible under the present restrictions of space. In order to point out the nature and extent of these movements, it will be sufficient to select a number of publications which have appeared in several countries. The huge number of publications does not imply great diversity, however; and it by no means implies genuine fruitfulness in many of the cases, especially in the field of existentialism. As in the first part of this survey, acknowledgment is made to scholars who contributed materials for their countries.

I. Germany

A. PHENOMENOLOGY[1]

The fact of Edmund Husserl's "non-Aryan" descent, as well as the rigorous method he endeavored to promote, will

[1] With acknowledgment to Professor Ludwig Landgrebe.

explain the almost total neglect of phenomenology in Germany following 1933. The number of recent publications on phenomenology could not be expected to be large. A generation of scholars who were either silenced or who could not come to the fore has now begun to review the past, and to look to Germany's best pre-Nazi achievements for renewed inspiration and orientation. Those writers on philosophy who came to terms with the Nazi régime, and whose writings echoed Nazi doctrines and bias, even to the extent of including passages from Alfred Rosenberg in technical philosophical treatises, are presented with a new problem of readjustment, which may well overtax the semantical possibilities of the German language. It seems safe to predict that the irrationalistic possibilities of existentialism rather than the descriptive ideal of phenomenology will provide the medium. That Ernst Cassirer's name could be stricken from the list of German philosophers at the 1937 Paris meeting of the International Congress of Philosophers, in the name of the Third *Reich;* that various philosophers could join the Nazi Party, with its implicit conduct and attitude, or could come to terms with Nazi cultural philosophy, with the rejection of the ideal of "objectivity" in science and philosophy; that Oskar Becker, easily one of Husserl's best equipped and ablest students a generation ago, could speak of "blood and earth" while discoursing of "transcendence and para-transcendence": these are samples of the ways in which some scholars accommodated themselves to the Nazi régime.

It may well be that the new edition of Husserl's *Erfahrung und Urteil*[2] will stimulate interest in phenomenological research in Germany. This important book was published in Prague in 1938, but because of the invasion

[2] Edited by Ludwig Landgrebe (Hamburg: Claasen and Goverts Verlag, 1948). See Supplement A, p. 229 of this book.

of the Nazis was lost except for two hundred copies sent
to England in time. Ludwig Landgrebe's *Phänomenologie
und Metaphysik*[3] is sure to resume contact with the tradition of phenomenology. As one of Husserl's former research
assistants, and with extensive experience in working on
Husserl's manuscripts, Professor Landgrebe is ideally
equipped to interpret phenomenology for a new generation of scholars. Introducing the book is a memorial address
for Husserl, delivered in 1938. Landgrebe considers the
"philosophy of life" of Dilthey and the philosophy of Heidegger in his attempt to show the methodological possibilities in Husserl's phenomenology for the purposes of a new
foundation of metaphysics. The phenomenological concept
of essence and essential intuition, the concept of a world,
as well as the relationship of Husserl's phenomenology to
Heidegger's philosophy, are discussed. The latter is conceived as a relationship of "mutual supplementation." The
phenomenological reduction is regarded not only as a preparatory methodological step, but as the method of metaphysics itself; the author undertakes to sketch the methodological possibilities of a phenomenological metaphysics.

Landgrebe's "Was bedeutet uns heute Philosophie"[4] was
intended as an introduction for a larger public. Philosophy
is portrayed not as an arbitrary succession of conflicting
systems, but a function belonging to the essence of human
existence. The origin of Greek philosophy is regarded as
the first great revolution of the Western spirit. It is taken
to signify the attempt to found the meaning of its existence
as knowledge. The second revolution, beginning with the
modern period, allows knowledge to be a tool of human

[3] (Hamburg: Marion von Schröder Verlag, 1948).
[4] (Hamburg: Marion von Schröder Verlag, 1948).

existence. It is held to lead in the last analysis to the abandonment of objective truth and to the European nihilism predicted by Nietzsche. In order to overcome it philosophy has the task, according to the writer, of restoring the original meaning of knowledge as the way of connecting human existence to its ground of being.

Eugen Fink's lecture, "Vom Wesen des Enthusiasmus,"[5] is also concerned with problems of the "essential transcendence of man," in the field of thought opened up by Husserl and Heidegger. Enthusiasm is not analyzed psychologically by him, but is examined for its "ontological significance." As the highest possibility of human existence, in which it is *"entrückt"* out of itself, enthusiasm is held to be the experience of that which *is* most (*"des am meisten Seienden—Theion"*) and, as such, the origin of the three "absolute relationships" in which man participates at the ground of being of all that is: of religion, art, and philosophy. These are viewed as being not only phenomena of human expression, as "objectivations" of the human spirit, but as the modes of the finite self-transcendence (*Selbstüberschreitung*) of finitude, the self-sacrifice of human freedom in yielding to the divine. In this conception of philosophy Fink goes along with the movement of contemporary German thought, in which philosophy is concerned, not as the freely creative work of man, but as an instrument of transcendence. Like Landgrebe, Fink was for years active as Husserl's assistant, and, again, on the preparation of Husserl's manuscripts for publication. Also like Landgrebe, who is oriented to *"Lebensphilosophie"* and to Heidegger's philosophy, Fink is receptive to other influences.[6] The

[5] (Freiburg i.B.: Chamier Verlag, 1947).

[6] That this tendency was adumbrated in the period of Fink's close association with Husserl was evident in his early writings.

190   THE AIMS OF PHENOMENOLOGY

"pure" phenomenology of Edmund Husserl has obviously
been continued in a rather mixed atmosphere.

The phenomena of "Simple Morality" has been analyzed
by Otto Friedrich Bollnow.[7] Since the great ethical systems
had failed to be convincing, following the loss of the comprehensive metaphysical world-view on which each one
was based according to Bollnow the ethical reflection must
begin with the question which generally accepted rules of
natural morality are still vital in the consciousness of even
the average man. Sympathy and "decency" are investigated as examples of immediate natural morality. It is the
task of ethics today, according to Bollnow, to connect with
these original moral and generally accepted impulses, to
show their meaning and justification, and thus to attain
"from below" to a more comprehensive ethics. Basic ideas
toward such an ethical philosophy are advanced in his
book, *Die Ehrfurcht*.[8]

Erich Rothacker's *Kulturanthropologie*[9] derives from
Dilthey's thought, but is also strongly influenced by phenomenology. It undertakes to supplement philosophical
anthropology by the investigation of man, insofar as he is
a carrier of culture; and also to carry the analysis of principles of culture to their origin in basic structures in the
essence of man. It proceeds from the relationship of man
to his environment, which is held to be different in principle from that of an animal, for man is not only adapted
to his environment, but masters it in a creative manner.
A specific human attitude arises in this mastery, which can
be recognized as the particular style of an epoch. Cultural
anthropology thus involves the reduction of all concepts,

[7] *Einfache Sittlichkeit* (Göttingen: Vandenhock und Rup-
precht, 1947).
[8] (Frankfurt a.M.: Klostermann, 1947).
[9] (Bonn: Bouvier Verlag, 1948).

with which the phenomena of human culture are interpreted, to the basic structures of man as a being existing in a world.

B. EXISTENTIALISM[10]

In the period following the war, existentialism came to occupy the central position on the philosophical scene. After its development in France, in connection with the earlier works of Heidegger and Jaspers, a strong movement returned to Germany at the close of the war. Such literary works as Sartre's *Flies* and Anouilh's *Antigone* were most prominent. They were performed on the German stage and discussed in the newspapers and periodicals, although the professional philosophers were relatively reticent. Thus, at the philosophical congresses in Garmisch-Partenkirchen in 1947, and in Mainz in 1948, there were no representative spokesmen for existentialism.

The articles which appeared were for the most part a report of French existentialism, rather than an independent development. There was no comprehensive treatment of the subject. Egon Vietta published a book entitled *Versuch über die menschliche Existenz in der modernen französischen Philosophie*,[11] which develops the Sartrean conception of existence, especially from his *La nausée*, and also discusses it critically from Heidegger's standpoint. Of the numerous articles in periodicals, mention may be made of articles by Bollnow[12] and Weischedel as more strictly

[10] With acknowledgment to Professor Otto Friedrich Bollnow.

[11] (Hamburg, 1948).

[12] "Existentialismus," *Die Sammlung*, II (1947) 654 ff.; "Albert Camus, Die Pest," *Die Sammlung*, III, (1948) 105 ff.; "Deutsche Existenzphilosophie und französischer Existentialismus," *Zeitschrift für philosophische Forschung*, II (1948), 231 ff; "Gabriel Marcel, Christlicher Existentialismus," *Die Sammlung*, III (1948), 400 ff., 481 ff., 549 ff.; "Zur Diskussion

philosophical.[13] Along with the growth of religious interest, the question of the possible union of existentialism and Christianity became more prominent. Existentialism faced the danger of being discredited as "dangerous" before it was examined. Theodore Steinbüchel, who died recently, published *Existentialismus und christliches Ethos*,[14] and Peter Wust's little book, *Der Mensch und die Philosophie: Einführung in die Existenzphilosophie*,[15] was selected from his literary remains for publication. It is worth noting that Wust explicitly uses the name "philosophy of existence," in the title of his book, for philosophy deriving from Catholicism and the scholastic tradition.

Heidegger appears to have refrained from publishing since the close of the war, although he is said to have prepared extensive manuscripts. Only his "Brief über den 'Humanismus'" has appeared, which he added to the reprinted edition of his *Platons Lehre von der Wahrheit*.[16] This letter, originally a reply to a letter from Jean Beaufret and thus itself a sign of the meeting of German and French philosophy, was published only in Switzerland and was therefore difficult to obtain in Germany. Although obscurely written, so that it is often difficult to take it literally, it is significant in that it represents a new departure for Heidegger. He sees the beginning of a false development in Plato and goes back to the pre-Socratic thinkers. Thus he appears to have turned toward a direct relation-

---

über die Existenz-philosophie auf dem philosophischen Kongress in Garmisch-Partenkirchen," *Zeitschrift für philosophische Forschung*, II (1948), 587 ff.

[13] Wilhelm Weischedel, "Das Anliegen des Existentialismus," *Pandora* (1948), pp. 3 ff.; "Wesen und Grenzen der Existenzphilosophie," *Frankfurter Hefte*, III (1948), 726 ff., 804 ff.

[14] (Heidelberg, 1948).

[15] (Münster, 1946).

[16] (Bern, 1947).

ship to being, and away from his earlier view that the ontology of human existence is prior to all other ontologies. Language is regarded by him as "the house of being," so that language and philosophical questions are accorded crucial importance.

After years of silence, because of the Nazi régime, Jaspers has returned to a position of prominence in the German philosophical world. His main work is the first volume of his "Philosophical Logic," entitled *Von der Wahrheit*.[17] This large work of more than 1000 pages presents the general bases for the volumes to come. In opposition to the modern irrationalistic prejudice against the supposed rigidity of concepts, as maintained by the "Philosophies of Life" and also in the beginning period of existentialism, Jaspers attempts to find a deeper ground for the function of logic in the whole of human existence. Logical-methodological questions are included in the comprehensive whole of a philosophy of existence. That is the meaning of the "philosophical logic" envisioned by Jaspers, with a certain reference to the Hegelian concept of logic, and with a certain parallelism to the program of a "hermeneutic logic" undertaken by Hans Lipps. The doctrine of the "Comprehensive" (*des "Umgreifenden"*) is of central importance, a doctrine developed by Jaspers in his *Vernunft und Existenz* in 1935, and taken over in the present work. Jaspers seeks by means of this basic concept to determine the common medium which emerges differently on the different levels of human existence (as existence, consciousness in general, spirit) as well as of extra-human being (as world and as transcendence). The concept of reason, which was dominant as late as the eighteenth century but was undermined by modern irrationalism, is

[17] *Philosophische Logik*, I, *Von der Wahrheit* (München, 1947).

again taken up in the frame of an existential philosophy.[18]

The way in which Jaspers views the relationship between existential philosophy and a special science of man is shown by the completely revised edition of his *Allgemeine Psychopathologie*.[19] Perhaps even more sharply than earlier he emphasizes a positivistic concept of science, which draws a clear line between the empirical investigation of facts and the existential attitude.

Der Philosophische Glaube,[20] by Jaspers, continues the tendency toward positive Christianity which was already shown by his *Nietzsche und das Christentum*.[21] Within philosophy itself he comes to recognize certain elements of belief, such as the existence of God and the existence of an unconditioned demand; but he also develops the painful experience of a gap between the basically tolerant openness of the philosophical attitude and the theological claim to absoluteness. Among the smaller writings and articles by Jaspers, some of which appeared in the periodical *Die Wandlung*, which he helped to found, was his speech of acceptance of the Frankfurt Goethe prize.[22] In it, the two-sidedness of his own position is indicated: there is the consciousness of an obligation to the great tradition, but there is also recognition of its uniqueness and of the necessity of a new beginning. It should be recalled that Jaspers, in the years following the war, has become the embodiment of a reawakened German spirit, both within and outside of Germany; and he has entered into more general

[18] See Section III for further discussion of Jaspers' conception of existentialism.

[19] (Berlin and Heidelberg, 1946).

[20] (München, 1948).

[21] (Güterslon, 1946).

[22] "Unsere Zukunft und Goethe," *Die Wandlung*, II, no. 7 (1947), 559 ff.

political discussions. His widely read little book, *Die Schuldfrage*,[23] and his Geneva lecture, *Vom europäischen Geist*,[24] belong here, as well as his contributions toward the reconstruction of the German university.[25]

Among the younger German existential philosophers, Gerhard Krüger has grown in prominence. In his various publications[26] in opposition to the ever stronger dissolution of all historical traditions and in opposition to the absolute freedom of man to make of himself what he will, emphasized by existentialism, he appears to seek to establish the authority of a binding tradition. Human freedom is restricted therewith to a limited area. Krüger's philosophy approaches evangelical theology. Also on the theological side, Helmut Thielicke may be mentioned as being close to the existentialist view in his treatment of the problem of death.[27]

In the borderline field of psychological investigation, two names have appeared recently in German-speaking Switzerland, and have met with attention. Wilhelm Keller endeavors in a Zürich lecture[28] to show the positive character of the concept of existence, and to gain thereby the

[23] (Heidelberg, 1946).

[24] (München, 1947).

[25] *Die Idee der Universität* (Berlin, 1946); "Erneuerung der Universität," *Die Wandlung*, I (1945), 66 ff.; "Volk und Universität, *Die Sammlung*, II, 54 ff.

[26] *Die Geschichte im Denken der Gegenwart* (Frankfurt a.M., 1947); *Leibniz als Friedensstifter* (Wiesbaden, 1947); "Christlicher Glaube und modernes Denken," *Studium Generale*, I (1948), 189 ff.; *Geschichte und Tradition, Lebendige Wissenschaft*, (Stuttgart, 1948); "Christlicher Glaube und existentielles Denken," *Festschrift für Rudolf Bultmann* (1949).

[27] *Tod und Leben: Studien zur christlichen Anthropologie* (2d ed., Tübingen, 1946).

[28] *Der positive Begriff der Existenz*.

basis for a sound methodological foundation of psychology. The second writer, Hans Kunz, published a large two-volume work, *Die anthropologische Bedeutung der Phantasie*.[29] Closely connected with the foundation provided by Heidegger, but also in complete independence, a philosophical elucidation of fantasy and of creative language is developed, concerned with the connections between nothing, death, and creative spirit. The inner connection between longing for distance and "homesickness for the origin" leads to the final questions of human existence.

The line of development of existential philosophy left unfinished by Hans Lipps as a result of his death is again undertaken by Bollnow in the essay on *Die Ehrfurcht* already mentioned. Some portions of the same writer's *Einfache Sittlichkeit*, dealing with the understanding of one's self and of others, connect with existential-philosophical lines of thought.

II. Holland and Belgium

A. PHENOMENOLOGY[30]

The presence of the Husserl Archives[31] in Louvain, under the direction of Herman Van Breda, and of the archives of Edith Stein[32] (since 1945), added greatly to the interest in phenomenology in Belgium and Holland.

[29] Part I, *The Psychological Analysis and Theory of Phantasy;* Part II, *The Anthropological Interpretation of Phantasy and its Presuppositions* (Basel, 1946).

[30] With acknowledgment to Professor J. Nota, S.J.

[31] Cf. *Philosophy and Phenomenological Research*, VII, no. 3 and VIII, no. 2, for Van Breda's account of the Husserl Archives.

[32] Husserl's assistant in the period of the First World War, who later became Schwester Benedicta a Cruce.

The remarkable story of the saving of Husserl's manuscripts, of their removal from Freiburg to Louvain under difficult and dangerous conditions, is testimony at the same time to the sagacity of Mrs. Edmund Husserl and to the resourcefulness and devotion of Herman Van Breda. The editorial work on the thousands of pages comprising the manuscripts continued during the Nazi occupation, and made rapid progress in the years following the war.

The most important Dutch publications were: A. Kievits, *Ethiek en religie in de philosophie van N. Hartmann* (see 1947 in the appended bibliography), which deals particularly with the ethics of Hartmann and his philosophy of religion; J. Nota, *Max Scheler* (see 1947), which undertakes to discover the unity of the continually changing and often contradictory thought of Scheler in his endeavor to attain to the nature of man. One also finds here a systematic account of phenomenology, especially concerning Husserl, with a full bibliography of Scheler and his works. Among the articles on phenomenology, the writings of S. Strasser are always important. Dr. Strasser was formerly connected with the Husserl Archives in Louvain, and is at present professor of philosophy in Nijmegen.

The first publication of the Edith Stein Archives was her *Wege der Gotteserkenntnis* (see 1946).

The following works, not historical but original, are each of conspicuous interest in their way: F. de Buytendijk, *Allgemene theorie der menselijke houding en beweging* (see 1948), interesting not only for the new manner of treating the subject, but also for its peculiar conception of empirical philosophy; also A. Snoeck, *De psychologie van het schuldbewustzijn,* which seeks to find a synthesis of the consciousness of guilt, after treating the conceptions of Freud, Scheler, Stoker, Jankélévitch, and others, and discussing the investigations undertaken by others and by himself.

Bibliography of Phenomenology in Holland, 1945–1948
(Tijdschrift voor Philosophie is abbreviated throughout to TP)

1945

Breda, H. van, "Hedendaagsche phenomenologische strooming," TP, VII (1945), 195–202. (Concerning the Husserl Archives in Louvain)

Strasser, S., "Het vraagstuk van het solipsisme bij Edmund Husserl," TP, VII (1945), 3–18. (The question of solipsism)

1946

Stein, Edith, *Wege der Gotteserkenntnis: Die "symbolische Theologie" des Areopagiten und ihre sachlichen Voraussetzungen,* Met inleiding van L. Gelber, namens E. Steinarchief te Leuven, TP, VIII (1946), pp. 27–74. (The symbolic theology of the Pseudo-Dionysius and its presuppositions, published by the Edith Stein Archives of Louvain)

Strasser, S., "Beschouwingen over het vraagstuk van de apodicticiteit en de critische verantwoording van de phenomenologie," TP, VIII (1946), 226–270. (On the question of the apodicticity and the justification of phenomenology)

1947

Buytendijk, F. *Het kennen van de innerlijkheid* (Nijmegen: Dekker v.d. Vegt, 1947). (Inaugural lecture at Utrecht: Knowledge of interiority)

Buytendijk, F., *De eerste glimlach van het kind* (Nijmegen: Dekker v.d. Vegt, 1947). (Inaugural lecture at Nijmegen: A child's first smile)

Haecht, L. van, *Taalphilosophische beschouwingen* (Louvain: Uitgaven van het hoger institut voor wijsbegeerte, 1947). (On linguistic philosophy)

Kieviets, A., *Ethiek en religie in de philosophie van N. Hartmann* (Nijmegen: Dekker v.d. Vegt, 1947).

Nota, J., *Max Scheler: Een worstelen om het wezen van den mens* (Utrecht-Brussels: Spectrum, 1947). (The anthropology of Max Scheler, with a disgression on phenomenology in general)

Redeker, H., "Een psycholoog in Heideggers voetsporen" (A. Kunz), TP, IX (1947), 465–472. (A psychologist in conformity to Heidegger)

Strasser, S., *Objectiviteit en objectivisme* (Nijmegen: Dekker v.d. Vegt, 1947). (Inaugural lecture at Nijmegen)

1948

Buytendijk, F., *Algemene theorie der menselijke houding en beweging* (Utrecht: Spectrum, 1948). (General theory of the attitude and movements of man)

Delfgaauw, B., "Heidegger en Sartre," TP, X (1948), 289–337, 403–446.

Snoeck, A., *De psychologie van het schuldbewustzijn* (Utrecht: Spectrum, 1948). (The psychology of the consciousness of guilt)

B. EXISTENTIALISM IN HOLLAND[33]

Because of the German occupation, communication with foreign countries was largely impossible, and hardly anyone in Holland even knew the name of Sartre as a philosopher. Until the middle of 1945, one could find only one copy of *L'Être et le Néant* in Holland. As a result of the lack of paper, large publications were impeded, especially during the first year after the liberation in May, 1945. R. F. Beerling's publication was the first one: *Moderne doodsproblematiek:een vergelijkende studie over Simmel, Heidegger, en Jaspers.*[34] The problem of death is treated in this book. In the introduction to his thesis, starting with the social situation of the nineteenth century, Beerling

[33] With acknowledgment to Professor H. Plessner.
[34] Diss. (Amsterdam, 1945).

explains the idea of death as individualism, which is at the same time a reaction against the individualism of the contented bourgeois of the nineteenth century. According to Beerling, the philosophy of existence is a product of the modern Crisis, which must be gone through before man can find his place again. In the three chapters on Simmel, Heidegger, and Jaspers, Beerling gives chiefly the important texts with some critical remarks, but without any final conclusion. For Simmel, death is the stimulation of life; it annihilates individuality, but is at the same time the principle of individuality. For Heidegger, death is an excitation of authenticity, although death gives no other perspective than itself. With quotations from Hegel and Husserl, Beerling criticizes the emotionality of the Heideggerian philosophy, which rejects any other interpretation of "existence" than through anguish, and which neglects the mind. According to Jaspers, it is death which separates the essential from the adventitious.

B. M. Delfgaauw has entitled his dissertation on Lavelle *Het spiritualistisch existentialisme van L. Lavelle*,[35] maintaining that Lavelle is also an "existentialist," because he starts with the concrete situation of the ego, and sees in existence the possibility of essence. He gives a detailed exposition of the work of Lavelle, with many quotations. At the end he criticizes the ambiguity of the words used by Lavelle, for instance "être," which is both the Absolute Being and the "étant," and he points out what appears to him to be the fundamental difficulty encountered by Lavelle's thought: What is man, if God is Being? He also gives a brief description of Lavelle's thought in an article in a Dutch philosophical periodical.[36] His book on the

[35]Diss. (Amsterdam, 1947).

[36] De wijsbegeerte van L. Lavelle," *Algemeen Nederlands Tijdschrift voor Wijsbegeerts en Psychologie* (1947), pp. 75–83.

philosophy of existence[37] is a short introduction in which
he treats in a hundred pages the most important existentialists, including G. Marcel, for example, and their forerunners, Kierkegaard and Nietzsche. The author does not
venture to offer any new ideas on the philosophy of existence. In an inaugural lecture entitled *Existentiele verwon-
dering* (1947), he deals with the problem of wonder about
being; he considers the ontological conceptions of Heidegger, Jaspers, and Sartre, and finally turns back to St.
Thomas and Hegel.

In cooperation with H. Robbers, Delfgaauw has published *Praeadviezen over existentialisme*.[38] After a brief
recapitulation of Kierkegaard, Marcel, and Jaspers by
Robbers, and of Nietzsche, Heidegger, and Sartre by Delfgaauw, the question of the relationship between Christianity and existentialism is raised. Robbers is able to accept
the existentialism of the first three, inasmuch as that would
not be opposed to Christianity (Catholicism), although he
prefers a more objective philosophy. Delfgaauw explains
the work of Heidegger and Sartre as an attempt at a synthesis of Hegel and Kierkegaard which miscarried; and he
hopes that Thomism will find this synthesis.

The thesis of C. A. van Peursen on the philosophy of
existence[39] is an effort to point out the character of risk in
this philosophy. Almost all the great systems are "magical";
choice, solitude, and death are forgotten. The value of the
philosophy of existence is held to lie in its renewal of the
question of the essence of man and his freedom. But this
"risking" philosophy does not provide any points of contact

[37] *Wat is existentiephilosophie?*, 1948.

[38] Vereniging to bevordering van de beoefening der weten-
schap onder de Katholieke in Nederland, 1947.

[39] *Riskante philosophie: een karakteristiek van het heden-
daagse existentiele denken* (Leiden, 1948).

with transcendence. It causes man to lose satisfaction with himself, but it does not necessarily lead to transcendence, which always springs from outside and suddenly. The philosophy of existence is only a window that overlooks the darkness, not a clear, wide road. Risk crushes our power, and we work for transcendence, without being able to force it to enter our world. Van Peursen has also written a brief introduction to existential philosophy,[40] which is merely intended to make known the ideas of these philosophers. And he has discussed the anthropology of the Swiss psychiatrist-philosopher, Binswanger, in an article.[41] Binswanger is accorded a much more "positive" place in the philosophy of existence than that of Heidegger and Sartre. The "me" and the "you" are united in a "we," a unity which is more than the sum of these two factors. Thus the philosophy of existence of Binswanger is, according to van Peursen, a true enrichment of existentialism.

J. B. Van der Weyden's book on existentialism[42] is a sketchy introduction with some critical remarks. But its appearance is another symptom of the interest of Holland in that philosophy, which in spite of and also because of many misunderstandings, continues to grow in prominence. This is also true of the two small publications of S. U. Zuidema,[43] *Nacht zonder dageraad* (Night without dawn) and *De mens als historie* (Man as History). The former disputes Sartre's ideas on the ground that he denies the existence of God and does not give any perspective. In the latter, the value of the philosophy of existence is recognized because it shows the historicity of man. But existentialism

[40] *Korte inleiding in de existentiephilosophie*, 1948.

[41] "De anthropologie van L. Binswanger en haar plaats binnen het kader der existentiephilosophie," *A.N.T.W.Ps.* (1948), pp. 177–184.

[42] *De stanboom van het existentialisme*, 1948.

[43] Inaugural lectures, 1948.

is, according to Zuidema, a philosophy of reduction, which must be unacceptable from the point of view of Protestant and orthodox theology.

An article by the Belgian scholar, A. de Waelhens,[44] may be mentioned here, because it is published in a Dutch philosophical periodical. It gives a brief portrayal of French existentialism: there is a description of Maine de Biran, Gabriel Marcel, Jean-Paul Sartre, and M. Merleau-Ponty, and the differences appear to be as great as the agreement.

In his pamphlet on existentialism and literature,[45] Dresden shows that the philosophy of existence has become important for the literary critic. The ideas of this philosophy and of literature are often the same (nothingness, anguish, death); but existential psychoanalysis is also, according to Dresden, the only adequate way to understand the writers, in view of its interest in the peculiar nature of each case. It is not jealousy in general, but this special jealousy of this writer, and how it is assimilated in the totality of his life, that makes us understand the writer and his works. In his article on Camus,[46] absurdity is regarded as paradoxical, because there is still an effort, even in the nihilism, which also becomes absurd.

Mention should also be made of the report of a symposium, held in 1946, which was organized to consider the problems of existentialism. In this symposium, Beerling characterizes existentialism as a humanism without any normative values, Debrot speaks of the relations between existentialism and the artistic, and the sociologist de Kadt describes existentialism as a symptom of decadence which can only arise in a society as rotten as ours.

[44] "Hoofdtrekken van het franse existentialisme," *A.N.T.W.Ps.* (1947).

[45] *Existentiephilosophie en litteratuurbeschouwing*, 1946.

[46] "A. Camus en de problematiek van het absurde," *Criterium* no. 405 (1945–1946).

The influence of the philosophy of existence extends also to theology, especially Protestant theology. The dissertation of J. Springer, *Argumentum ontologicum*,[47] discusses the famous proof of St. Anselm and gives it an existential interpretation, with respect to Jaspers' concept of a "cipher." It is only possible to understand this proof as a "cipher"; it is at the same time a prayer.

The study of Hoenderdaal on Schleiermacher[48] provides an example of this influence, precisely because existentialism is not treated there. But the separation of theology and aesthetics is denied and the possibility of the unity of the two in the human personality is maintained, in accordance with the philosophy of existence, notably with Jaspers. The relationship between religion and aesthetics is viewed as one between existence and reason (as *Vernunft*).

It is also easy to note the influence of the philosophy of existence in the field of psychiatry. The ideas of Jaspers and Heidegger play a big role in the large work of L. van der Horst and H. Hugenholtz.[49] But the influence of the existential philosophy on psychiatry is seen particularly in a study by J. H. van den Berg.[50] Here, the separation between philosophy (philosophical anthropology) and psychiatry is effaced. The "anthropology" of Heidegger, and especially of Binswanger, is of the greatest importance, according to the author, for the understanding of schizophrenia: one knows time, but without duration; a world, but without the being-with-others; etc. This is manifested

[47] (Groningen, 1947).

[48] *Religieuse existentie en aesthetische aanschouwing: een studie over het misverstand omtrent het aesthetisch element in Schleiermacher's wezensbepaling der religie*, diss. (Leiden, 1948).

[49] *Anthropologische Psychiatrie*, 1946–1947.

[50] *De betekenis van de phaenomenologische of existentiele anthropologie in de psychiatrie*, 1946.

by the patient's attitude, by his responses, etc. Is it possible by means of a phenomenological anthropology alone to understand such manifestations, and to answer the question: At what point of schizophrenia is one still a man?

The influence of the philosophy of existence is also seen in psychology. A book by C. W. du Boeuff and P. C. Kuiper[51] is again oriented toward Heidegger and Jaspers, in that the authors wish to overcome the separation of subject and object which has been so prominent since Descartes. Now it is necessary to "think-in-union," if one wishes really to understand the psychological phenomena. "Thinking-in-union" is supposed to take the place of "thinking-in-separation."

In his dissertation, *Psychologie van projectieverschijnselen*,[52] D. J. van Lennep finds that the philosophy of existence helps us to understand psychical projection. The work of Sartre appears to him to be especially fruitful, although the author declares expressly that his acceptance of the psychological ideas of Sartre does not imply the acceptance of his ontology. It is the psychological work (*Esquisse d'une Théorie des Émotions, L'Imaginaire*) to which he refers.

Finally, the inaugural lecture of F. J. Buytendijk[53] considers problems arising through the contact of psychology and philosophical anthropology. The boundaries between them are regarded as more or less obliterated, because introspection touches the "heart" of man, which is also manifested in communication with others. One knows another person only if one loves him, if one knows his existence (Scheler).

[51] *Waan en vervreemding: een anthropologische studie naar aanleiding van de melancholie*, 1946.

[52] (Utrecht, 1948).

[53] *Het kennen van de innerlijkheid*, 1947.

Existentialism did not become the fashion in Holland as it was in France after the war. But in theology (especially Protestant theology), in psychology, and in psychiatry, it became the most important subject of discussion. The influence of the existential philosophy on literature is promoted not only by the philosophical publications, but above all by the existentialist literature.

III. Three Existentialists

The four leading existentialists are Heidegger, Jaspers, Marcel, and Sartre. Heidegger's limited publication in this period has already been referred to (in Section I). It will be of interest to consider in somewhat greater detail one of Jaspers' attempts to present his version of existentialism, in connection with his fellow Christian-existentialist, Gabriel Marcel, and also with the "humanistic" attempt of Sartre. Since it is so common for existential philosophers to use strange epithets for their own work as well as other people's, and to proceed with great rapidity toward conclusions without regard to logical procedures, it should be in order to examine their texts for logical merit, as well as for their truth and significance.

A. KARL JASPERS ON THE PHILOSOPHY OF EXISTENCE[54]

In his discussion of "philosophical faith," Jaspers rejects the "facile alternatives" of "revealed faith or nihilism, of total science or illusion," declaring that they serve as weapons of spiritual intimidation. He appears to be eager

[54] Karl Jaspers, *The Perennial Scope of Philosophy*, trans. by Ralph Manheim (New York: Philosophical Library, 1949). Five of the six lectures comprising the volume were delivered at the University of Basel in 1947.

to overstate the case for scientific knowledge in such a way as to make room for another position which would escape the artificially introduced limitations. Thus, the spokesman for science is made to state that "apart from the sciences there are only illusions." For his part, Jaspers proposes "to keep open the horizons of humanity in our philosophical thinking." His attempt to make clear the nature of philosophical faith is hardly successful, even though he is obviously toying with old constructions—e.g., "this faith that comprehends subject and object." Faith is regarded as an immediate experience of the "Comprehensive" (i.e., the being that is neither only subject nor only object). If the reader is gratified at having reached a familiar and recognizable point, he soon learns that "the ground and primal source of our being seems to slip into the psychologically indescribable," which is curiously called "contingency."

Neither is the account of "transcendence" satisfactory. There is transcendence, in his view, "if the world does not consist only of itself, *is not built upon itself*, but points beyond itself" (italics mine). He recognizes clearly that "if the world is everything, then there is no transcendence." It is difficult to understand how a man of Jaspers' scientific training can say that "we take our life from a primal source that lies beyond the being-there . . . beyond consciousness and beyond mind"; and, again, "I know that I have been given to myself in transcendence." It seems appropriate that he introduces a vague notion of "dialectic" in order to provide a sanction for his irrationalistic trend. It is then possible to reconcile irreconcilables: for, "just as Being and Nothingness are inseparable, each containing the other, so faith and unfaith are inseparable. . . ." Jaspers' penchant for mystical language is shown when he speaks of compressing himself in his own shrinking self.

Although declaring that proofs for the existence of God

are "impossible," Jaspers holds that such arguments do not lose their validity as ideas because they have lost their power to prove. A certainty of the existence of God is regarded as a premise, not as a result of philosophical activity. He significantly states that "the futility of human designs and realizations . . . brings us to the edge of the abyss, where we experience nothingness or God." Evidently he has been deeply impressed by the frustrations of the past years, with the result that he has been led to accept a philosophy of defeat so far as the actual satisfaction of human needs is concerned. At any rate, such an ultimate fact as finitude should not be confused with the area of actual activity within which we can do much to insure the fulfillment of human designs.

It is not easy to understand how anyone with even a slight amount of intellectual power could convince himself of the doctrine of the "Absolute," which is held to exist as a foundation for action. This "Absolute" is an object of faith and not of knowledge; it "erupts from the Transcendent into this world by way of our freedom." What can a writer fancy that he is talking about when he uses such words? The recent war illustrated numerous "eruptions," but it is not possible to point to anything of the kind suggested here.

Jaspers appears to be confused when he argues that the world is not self-contained, and that it is not grounded in itself. This conclusion is at best a *non sequitur* after his preceding remarks. One does not have to judge the world one-sidedly or fallaciously; one does not have to judge "the world" at all. Jaspers has not indicated in any way how he arrives at his goal of regarding the world as "the meeting-point of that which is eternal and that which manifests itself in time."

The discussion of "man" is no more satisfactory. That there can be no human goodness without self-reflection

may well be partially true. But Jaspers clearly wanders
away from sound reasoning when he declares that "with
self-reflection goodness cannot be blameless and pure." He
even misses making it a neat epigram, for "blameless" and
"pure" are assumptive epithets. It is possible to be antiscientific even while seemingly allowing the special sciences their regions of validity. Jaspers criticizes the special
sciences which investigate the nature of man in so many
different ways or contexts. He holds that "the insights
remain scattered, do not combine into a complete synthesis." He objects to "total judgments of man" on the basis
of the special sciences, to "supposed understandings of the
whole." But how is this alleged defect to be remedied?
By having philosophical oracles mouth generic pronouncements about the "total" or "fundamental" nature of man?

Jaspers' antievolutionary view of man is consistent with
his general irrationalism. "Man cannot be derived from
anything else, but is immediately at the base of all things."
Curiously, to be aware of this signifies man's "freedom."
On the other hand, "every insight into man, if absolutized
into a supposed knowledge of man as a whole, destroys his
freedom." This is held to be the reason for the inadequacy
of psychoanalysis, Marxism, and racial theory. The indis-
criminate condemnation of such totally different views is
itself evidence of "standpoint" reasoning. Jaspers is sure
that "man as a whole can never become the object of
scientific investigation," and that "man is always more than
he knows about himself." It is also true that a table or a
stone are more than what is known about them. It would
seem to be clear that more science rather than nonscience
(i.e., irrationalism, or existentialism) is required.

The concept of "transcendence" plays a decisive role
for Jaspers. Man's self is regarded as a free gift to him by
transcendence; and "transcendent help reveals itself to
him solely in the fact that he can be himself." The religious

nature of transcendence is clearly avowed, for the fact that man can stand by himself is declared due to an intangible hand, extended to him "from transcendence," a hand "whose presence he can feel only in his freedom." Now, "man as freedom" is a matter of faith, not knowledge. What, then, can one think of Jaspers' contention (it can hardly be reassuring, under the circumstances) that "it is only through freedom that I become certain of transcendence"? Since "freedom" is based upon faith, it follows that the "certainty" is a matter of faith.

The idea that all men are equal is declared to be "obviously false," not only psychologically, but also "considered as the reality of a social order." The best that he is able to do is repeat the Kantian principle that one should not be treated only as a means.

A curtain of ignorance is drawn over science when it is declared that man "cannot adequately account for his sojourn in the world by the laws immanent to the world." The "primal source" of man is sought "beyond the world." The "awakened man" is characterized by "existential anguish." Playing again the old theme of the limitations of scientific knowledge, Jaspers declares that one must not expect of science what it can never achieve—*viz.*, one cannot live by it, as an "absolute." What he finds so necessary for living is something which only "metaphysical meanings" can provide, "a sense of contentment with being." But, it will be asked, why contentment precisely? Why not *discontentment* with particular conditions of "being"? "Repose" is not necessarily what one really wants. It would seem to be desirable to use all the scientific knowledge we can gain, in order to adjust "being" to us, and ourselves to "being," for the greatest possible achievement of values. One should not lose oneself in generalities, and become so much absorbed in a general ontological problem (assuming that it is a real problem) that he fails to note biological and social problems of adjustment and the achievement of values.

Jaspers' further presentation shows him to move within the very familiar framework of a religious philosophy. In the course of his discussion of philosophy and religion he remarks that without authority no human life is possible. Because an individual is "finite, particular, and one-sided," the church is "a spokesman for the collectivity." The "philosophical faith" which is extolled, the faith which provides "living contact with the Comprehensive," is "built upon authority." He asserts sententiously that no one can lay a foundation other than that which has been laid down from the beginning. He is sure that the authoritative guidance provided by the past cannot be formulated in objective, universally binding terms. How then can he expect acceptance of it? Carried along by his quite uncritical enthusiasm, he finds that "any meaningful philosophy must develop in this authority." It is hardly necessary to refer to the conflicting elements in the historical tradition to show that Jaspers' account is just as "existentially empty" as he accuses certain others of being. Nominalism and realism, rationalism and empiricism, idealism and materialism: these largely conflicting trends will not fit into the one-sided scheme of philosophy portrayed by him.

But Jaspers is prepared to ward off this criticism in his discussion of "philosophy and anti-philosophy." The defense of his otherwise patently untenable position consists in the very simple device of defining "philosophy" to suit his purpose, and in the use of the convenient designation of "anti-philosophy." The philosophy which turns against "philosophy" in his sense is termed "anti-philosophy," and is called "the negation of philosophy." Like the weakness of Adam, this germ of anti-philosophy is present in everyone. Fortunately, however, the reader is fully equipped with the means to overcome this difficulty. Like Pegasus, only far more powerful, the concept of transcendence is at hand (or, more exactly, the *word* "transcendence," which is quite enough in the present uncritical context). Thus, a philosophically inclined man becomes a philosopher by "transcending" the anti-philosophy that is always present in himself.

The three examples of anti-philosophy (all of them examples of "unbelief," which "is never in contact with being") chosen for examination are demonology, the deification of man, and nihilism. In accordance with "demonologism," the gods themselves "have become world," and are held to participate in the impotence of the world. In a word, "it misses transcendence." The deification of man turns out to be one kind of demonology, and Jaspers contends that there is in the world no man capable of being God for us. Greatest interest attaches to "the open unbelief known as nihilism." For the nihilist there is no absolute, no being as such; everything is questionable. Determined to paint a picture of a perfect horror, Jaspers goes on to say, "nothing is true, everything is permissible." About whom can he be speaking? Examples of "nihilistic negation" are as follows: there is no God; there is no relationship between God and man; there is no obligation toward God. Such a nihilistic view "seems to regard being as identical with empirical existence, which can be fully known." Along with this view, according to Jaspers, there goes the "presupposition" that the ordering of human life can be derived from the knowledge of empirical realities— in other words, by means of scientific knowledge. He is clearly unfair in his criticism of this "presupposition," for he selects sex relations as an example, and supposes the view in question to maintain that "sex relations are to be regulated according to principles of hygiene with a view to realizing the aim of a happy life, without further religious or ethical considerations." He objects to the "premise" of the absolute character of a "mere life," and he believes that "happiness" cannot be clearly defined. The example of sex relations is no doubt chosen to arouse hostility; and the suggestion that the principles of hygiene alone are to be the guide is clearly an unfounded one, inasmuch as there is no responsible scholarly exponent of such a position. Jaspers has simply manufactured a standpoint for his convenience, but since the standpoint in question has no defenders, he has won a doubtful victory. That "happiness" is difficult to define, everyone will allow who has reflected upon it. That it cannot be "clearly defined" is, however, again an unwarranted *ad hoc* assumption.

All three positions—demonology, the deification of man, and nihilism—are disposed of as fallacious in one stroke of the pen. They "vanish like mist beneath the sun" in the presence of the proposition: God is. God is "transcendence," but God "can never be really apprehended." This is, in effect, a negative theology.

Jaspers turns finally to the consideration of the philosophy of the future. After sketching the unhappy conflicts and the great suffering of the past and of recent years, as well as the great changes in attitude that have resulted, he asks whether all this is a spiritual revolution, or "an essentially external process, arising from technology and its consequences." The way in which the question is put and the use of assumptive terms ("an essentially *external* process") indicate the fideistic view of Jaspers. But this is a scientific question of causal analysis, and not a matter of "philosophical faith," which means essentially, of preconceived ideas. Jaspers' antecedent store of ideas, perhaps partly unconscious, may be inferred as he goes along in his argument. Thus, he lashes out at "mass education," which, he declares, has made men "blind and thoughtless, capable of everything in their drunkenness." Can anyone seriously suggest that mass education was responsible for the terrible Nazi régime? Not even miseducation alone could explain that ill-fated régime or, indeed, any of the other major evils of the present world; it is at most an auxiliary factor. If one avoids positive causes, and refuses to recognize conflicting interests as causal factors, he can only look to "spiritual" explanations.

Jaspers' portrayal of philosophy is certainly one-sided. No one will deny him the privilege of asserting his personal view; but one may with right deny him the privilege of speaking for philosophy in general. He believes that philosophy is concerned with attaining "the meaning of life beyond all worldly purposes," that the enduring task of philosophy is "to become ourselves by achieving certainty of God," and that peace of mind is the aim of philosophical thought.

Before closing his discussion, Jaspers has occasion to give recognition to scientific method. His brief description of the scientific method leaves little to be desired, so far as it goes, but it comes too late, and it yields to his ulterior beliefs. His warning against "superstitious belief in science" is reminiscent of many popular religious and idealistic criticisms of science. As against his line of reasoning, it may be argued that there is no assignable limit to scientific inquiry. It need not be said that "science is everything," for, taken literally, it is not. But it is true that nothing is *per se* exempt from scientific (or logical) inquiry. A mysterious "transcendence" which cannot be embraced by the field of science has a dubious status, if it is not simply meaningless.

Jaspers' book is disappointing: more could have been expected from a man of his scientific training. That he should have become a major source of existentialism, with growing influence in France (thus Gabriel Marcel acknowledges indebtedness to him with profound respect) and elsewhere, is indeed a sign of the times. The reader will hardly expect that the effects of his influence will exceed the cause in merit—and he will be correct.

B. GABRIEL MARCEL AND CHRISTIAN EXISTENTIALISM[55]

In close agreement with Jaspers, Marcel "points out" the restriction of the concept of man by historical materialism and by the Freudian doctrines. These two standpoints are as it were the twin devils to be warded off. Pausing to refer to his metaphysical distinction between the "full" and the "empty," which he holds to be more fundamental than the distinction between the "one" and the "many," Marcel goes on to arraign the sciences and the scientific view of the world. This is done in defense of "mystery." The category of the "purely natural" is declared to be "pseudo-scientific," and the atrophy of the "faculty of wonder" is said to result from its adoption.

What Marcel calls the "ontological need" cannot be defined completely, for "this need . . . can never be wholly clear to itself." His attempt to "describe" it is hardly satisfactory. "Being is—or should be—necessary," he writes. This is a curious thing to say, from any point of view. His dialectical argument concerning pessimism is pointless, for he has the pessimist say "it would be *well* if there were being [italics mine], but there is no being [why should the pessimist be made to add that?], and I . . . am therefore nothing." The issue expressed by pessimism involves con-

[55] Gabriel Marcel, *The Philosophy of Existence*, trans. by Manya Hari (New York: Philosophical Library, 1949). The first of the four essays of this volume, "On the Ontological Mystery," was written in 1933; the second, "Existence and Human Freedom" (Paris, 1946), is a critical survey of the philosophy of Sartre; the third, "Testimony and Existentialism," also written in 1946, presents Marcel's conception of existentialism; and the fourth, "An Essay in Autobiography," is taken from the volume *Existentialisme Chrétien*, edited by E. Gilson (Paris, 1947).

siderations both of value and existence. In any case, Marcel does very little to illuminate the nature of "the ontological need." One speaks of a need for food, for shelter, for cultural activities, etc. Can one speak meaningfully of a "need for being"? There is a need for continued being, but is there one for being as such? The ontological need is said to have an "indeterminate" character. In the course of his meditation on the nature of being, Marcel is suddenly aware of an abyss under his feet, and he reflects: "I who ask these questions about being, how can I be sure that I exist?" He does not believe that Descartes' *cogito* helps at this point.

Marcel's readiness to avow mystery where no mystery at all need be held to exist is seen in the alleged "mystery of cognition": "Knowledge is contingent on a participation in being for which no epistemology can account because it continually presupposes it." He would do well to remind himself of what Kant says in his *Critique of Pure Reason* about the art of asking the right questions. That knowledge occurs in the world is a basic fact, and there is no mystery connected with it, even though there is so much to analyze and so many problems remain to be solved.

The distinction between a "mystery" and a "problem" is not helpful. It would seem to be a general fact that whenever an existentialist is embarrassed for lack of a precise idea or standard, he invokes the aid of "transcendence" (N.B., the mystery of mysteries). Thus, "a mystery is a problem, which encroaches upon its own data . . . thereby transcending itself as a simple problem." The example of the "mystery of the union of body and soul" is hardly acceptable. Only a "loaded" concept of a soul could confer a mystery. The concept of a mystery is itself "loaded," so that it is placed beyond reach of all rational means. Evidently it belongs to a higher order than problems. Thus, the reader learns that "in reflecting on a mystery we . . . degrade it to the level of a problem." The aim is "by a way of liberation and detachment from experience" to rise to the level of "the meta-problematical and of mystery."

What is the starting point of metaphysics? A scientifically oriented person would surely think of the philosophical function of synthesis, and declare the special sciences to provide the essential basis for synthesis. Marcel, however, reveals his peculiarly nonscientific motivation when he states that "the fact that suicide is possible is the essential starting point of any genuine metaphysical thought." From this point on the going becomes ever more mysterious, involving a rapid succession of key terms which finally find a unity of expression and significance in the faith professed by the author. Despair, or "the act by which one despairs of reality as a whole" has at its basis the belief that there is no security in the realm of reality. Hope, on the other hand, involves the belief that "there is at the heart of being . . . a mysterious principle which is in connivance with me."

This brings Marcel to the center of what he calls the "ontological mystery"; but the illustration he introduces is revealing rather than convincing. If one expresses the hope that a person will recover from an incurable disease, that is to say that it is impossible that he should be alone in willing this cure (Why impossible? Might one be not alone in such a case?); and this in turn is held to imply that "it is impossible that reality in its inward depth [an engaging phrase, but thoroughly vacuous withal!] should be hostile or . . . indifferent. . . ." Either the entire thought process illustrated here is merely a hope, or it must remain a mystery how Marcel connects reality with human values. He does indeed recognize that the structure of the world we live in permits absolute despair, but he adds that "it is only such a world that can give rise to an unconquerable hope." The reader will have to let the matter stand as a hope. This might well be more acceptable if it presented a challenge, and an incentive for progress toward the solution of problems. But, unfortunately, that is not the kind of hope the author has in mind, for his hope is a mystery. Man can achieve as much as his "technics" will accomplish, but, Marcel maintains, "these technics are unable *to save man himself.*" He makes the much hackneyed point that "man is at the mercy of his technics," but he does not show why man is incapable of controlling his technical progress. Although he quotes the view that the optimism of technical progress is animated by great hope, he maintains that "the only genuine hope is hope in what does not depend on ourselves, hope springing from humility and not from pride." The contrast to the buoyant confidence in the capacity of scientific progress which was so prominent in the eighteenth century in France is striking. Marcel is obviously concerned with circumscribing the sphere of reason, making room for faith. His objective is certainly familiar, although his method of attack follows a devious route with numerous gaps in the argument.

The introduction of the idea of "creative fidelity" is typical of his procedure. This concept involves the idea of "presence," which is "mystery in the exact measure in which it is present." Since fidelity is "ontological," it "prolongs presence." Presence is described as more than the object, as exceeding the object on every side; and death appears as "the test of presence." The truth he is attempting to probe is "infinitely mysterious." A slight direction appears in Marcel's words when he describes creative fidelity as "maintaining ourselves actively in a permeable state." Following his play with the notions of "spiritual availability" and "unavailability," light finally breaks into the turbid text when he makes direct reference to Christianity. Thus, we may think of the Eucharist in connection with "presence" and of the Church in connection with creative fidelity. He concedes it to be quite possible that the existence of the fundamental Christian data may be necessary *in fact* to enable the mind to conceive of some of the notions he has attempted to analyze. Speaking to Catholics, Marcel affirms the distinction between the natural and the supernatural. Aware that he may be criticized for using the term "mystery," he maintains that he is able to distinguish clearly between "mysteries which are enveloped in human experience as such" and "mysteries which are revealed, such as the Incarnation or Redemption." He is convinced that there is, "in the depth of nature," and of reason, "a fundamental principle of inadequacy to itself"; and he believes that the "recognition of the ontological mystery" is only possible "through a sort of radiation which proceeds from revelation itself."

Referring to the first part of his well-known *Journal métaphysique*, Marcel states that his aim was to try to "discern the transcendental conditions of faith." Faith seemed to him to be "by its essence beyond all possible confirmation or disproof." He is careful to point out his opposition to a religion founded on reason, "beyond all confessional differences." No one will deny him the privilege of choosing his own religious denomination. It would be far better, however, to do so simply and deliberately, than to put forward a line of thought which its author admits is "difficult to paraphrase in concrete terms." There can be no belief in general, he points out. Belief is regarded as the attitude of a subject who is individual and concrete, but who is not the same as the empirical "I," for this "I" can be reduced to a set of objectively definable determinations. Would it not be far more simple, and correct, to say that beliefs always involve individual believers, who are historically conditioned and usually belong to organized traditions; and would not frankness require that one openly add his acceptance of one of these traditions? But that would render the entire matter "empirical," and capable of being accounted for in scientific terms, which would clearly be unwelcome to M. Marcel. He is sure that "the universe into which we have been thrown cannot satisfy our reason." In his essay on "Testimony and Existentialism" he maintains, on faith, that life is a gift, and that all things are given to one. It is a curious fact that he criticizes the man of Heidegger and Sartre who, "as the victim of some cosmic catastrophe, is flung into an alien universe to which he is bound by nothing," while himself speaking of being "thrown" into the universe. Presumably the last thing to expect from an existentialist is due awareness of the evolution of man and the universe. Marcel's conviction that reality cannot be "summed up" he owes in part to Bradley. Above all, it seems that Marcel loves a mystery. Appealing to experience, in opposition to empiricism, which "ignores the part of invention and . . . creative initiative," he refuses to take experience for granted and to ignore its "mystery." It cannot fail to be amazing that a man as gifted as Marcel finds it "amazing and miraculous that there should be experience at all."

Marcel's criticism of Sartre is by far the ablest portion of the volume. Through it all he is very sure of his own faith. Sartre appears to him to labor the term "transcendence," and it does not mean the right thing. Marcel, of course, knows what it properly means—the transcendence of a superior being. Sartre is "obscene," deliberately so, as Marcel frequently indicates. The reader is given a full opportunity to appreciate the "obscene" illustrations. If Sartre eschews tables and apples, hitherto favorite objects for philosophical elucidation, he revels in such things as sewer-pipes, excremental processes, or perversions. The reality in experience of his examples cannot be denied. Whether they are typical need not be argued, even on

Sartrean grounds. The important thing to decide is whether the structures in experience he is concerned with delineating have a real basis or not. That Sartre is also "intelligent," the reader is told repeatedly. Presumably there is a very narrow gate available to Sartre for a trip toward salvation (a Marcellian religious salvation). He is not only intelligent; he often makes striking observations and descriptive analyses. Only the latter are held to be erroneous, in crucial cases where matters of principle are involved; they exploit equivocations, are confused, or simply monstrous. Sartre is "audacious," moreover. As Marcel reacts to his own religious assurance, he seems to take on the tone of the medieval tradition he has adopted, and he chides Sartre with more "audacity" than has ever been evinced, in rejecting grace in every sense through his analysis of "gifts" and giving, and his doctrine of freedom. Marcel makes some good critical points in his analysis of Sartre's errors, and in exposing his loose usage, which is at times just as bad as the linguistic excesses of Hegel. He correctly sees one of Sartre's major obstacles to be the instatement of an ethical theory on the basis of his very strange ontology, or his theory of non-being, coupled with freedom. But he is hardly a saint of logic himself, and his own errors easily outweigh those of the vulnerable Sartre. His condemnation of "crass materialism" shows how he is capable of hurling epithets from a limited and biased point of view.

It is quite apparent that Marcel is primarily a fideist, a "standpoint philosopher," and his appeal will be almost exclusively to persons who are already convinced believers. He has numerous insights, both borrowed and original. But there is very little evidence of painstaking preparatory work, such as is characteristic of the genuine phenomenologist when he undertakes to clarify ideas by tracing them to their sources in experience. Marcel's text can be more readily followed when one is aware of his aversions and inclinations than by attempting to trace out any logical connections: against materialism and naturalism, against the scientific view of the world as the basis for a philosophy, against the exclusive use of logical procedures; for a supernatural, for a region inaccessible to reason—in short, for "transcendence" and his faith. Logical connections are largely conspicuous by their absence, and the pervasive irrationalism is partially concealed by the skillful use of special terms.

C. JEAN-PAUL SARTRE AND HUMANISTIC EXISTENTIALISM[56]

Sartre's lecture on *L'Existentialisme est un Humanisme,* delivered in Paris in 1945, was an attempt at a popular exposition of the central aim of his philosophy. There is in it none of the comparatively close thinking of his earlier phenomenological studies; also completely absent is the grand plan of the *L'Être et le Néant,* with its Cartesian and Hegelian, as well as phenomenological and existential, elements. Although it may not be considered a satisfactory statement of any aspect of his philosophy, it is nevertheless characteristic of his style of thinking. Its looseness and vagueness are not accidental; they are inherent in the position set forth, and they reflect a kind of irresponsible mode of reaction to unclarified motives. That a man of Sartre's unquestionable literary ability should misstate himself seriously is hardly plausible. This publication can only be regarded as revealing, even after all due allowance for the occasion and purpose has been made.

Surely little sense can be attached to the statement that by existentialism is meant "a doctrine which makes human

[56] Jean-Paul Sartre, *Existentialism,* trans. by Bernard Frechtman (New York: Philosophical Library, 1947).

life possible"? That would indeed be a great doctrine! That every action implies a human setting may well be true, although hardly informative; but that every *truth* implies a human setting and a human subjectivity, as Sartre asserts, may be disputed. There are objective scientific truths for which the human setting is simply irrelevant. The "human subjectivity" is important in connection with the phenomenological procedure, but care must be taken not to allow it to predetermine a metaphysics within the limits of subjectivity. The declaration that "subjectivity must be the starting point," which is meant to be an alternative statement for "existence precedes essence," aligns Sartre with the phenomenological procedure. The entire attempt to elucidate this idea is unsuccessful in the present account. How can it be said that "man is what he conceives himself to be"? Sartre wishes to point out the self-sufficiency of man and his non-dependence on a divine being. He would have done much better to let the matter rest with the denial of a supernatural cause, without going to the extreme of having a kind of mythical "man" who "wills himself to be" and "thrusts toward existence." Sartre's man "hurls himself toward a future." Some reading in the literature of evolution, and especially of cultural anthropology, might have a salutary effect on his thinking and writing.

It is unsatisfactory and confusing to call the principle of subjectivity the first principle of existentialism if that is taken to mean that "man is nothing else but what he makes of himself." If the reader has grasped this formulation of subjectivity, he is due for a jolt when he learns that the essential meaning of existentialism is "that it is impossible for man to transcend subjectivity."

Also unclear is the talk of a man being "responsible" for himself, in the sense of being responsible for all men. No reasons are given, although it appears that the writer has in mind the concept of man as a social being. It would be difficult to find a more unsatisfactory attempt to expound or justify an idea. It remains to be shown how an individual "chooses all men" when "choosing himself"; and it is necessary to elucidate his assertions that "we can never choose evil," and that "nothing can be good for us without being good for all." Although the emphasis on the social is praiseworthy, closely reasoned arguments should be expected, rather than more or less vague assertions and dogmatic pronouncements. All that Sartre has to show us in the present context is a kind of attenuated, cloudy reminiscence of Kant's categorical imperative.

Evidently Sartre regards the characteristic existentialist terms, "anguish," "forlornness," and "despair," as too precious to drop under any circumstances. The quaint assertion that "man is anguish" is taken to mean that one cannot help "choosing all mankind as well as himself." Why should this be called "anguish," precisely? Is it because there is so much tension when an avowedly individualistic philosophy overstretches itself to consider the good of society? It is hardly necessary to observe that regard for others, or for humanity as a whole, may be accompanied by just the opposite of "anguish." There may be states of tranquility, or of exhilaration, and agreeableness. As for forlornness, it appears to be retained out of fidelity to Heidegger. If it merely means that man has to face the consequences of God's non-existence, Sartre is making a damaging admission by his very usage. A self-sufficient naturalism, a vigorous humanism, a genuine optimism—none of these views could find a place for the alleged forlornness of man. The strange mixture which Sartre calls "existentialism" seems to have something for everybody, and the many perplexed people of our time will find it reassuring to know that forlornness is a concept with real ontological depth.

Man is said to be "condemned to be free"; and the reader
is again reminded that man is "thrown into the world."
This language is closer to the fallen-angel concept of man
than to the risen-animal view of evolutionary naturalism.
Despair, too, has a "very simple meaning," *viz.*, that we are
confined "to reckoning only with what depends upon our
will, or on the probabilities which make our action possible." Certainty concerning the future may well be impossible. In fact, the argument could be extended to empirical
knowledge in general, which is a matter of probability, if
one cares to press the point. There is no need for "despair,"
however, in view of the great success of our empirical
knowledge, and, in particular, of our predictions. Mortality
studies are remarkably reliable. One can easily overempha-
size the aspect of uncertainty, and despair when there is no
need for despair.

The Cartesian *cogito*, or the subjectivity of the individual, is the point of departure for Sartre. Outside the *cogito*,
"all views are only probable." This is not a tenable statement, however, for mathematical (deductive) knowledge
is not limited to the *cogito*, and is irrelevant to it. Furthermore, probability estimates are objective and rigorous,
within the limits either of a formal theory or of a clearly
delimited set of facts. It is misleading, to say the least, to
assert that "a doctrine of probability which is not bound
to a truth dissolves into thin air," and that "in order to
describe the probable, you must have a firm hold on the
true." No alleged "absolute truth" is needed, apart from
the logical relations among propositions, and these have no
reference to the *cogito*. As the present writer has shown
elsewhere,[57] the method of Cartesian doubt is nugatory,

[57] Cf. the present writer's essay, "Experience and Subjectivism," in *Philosophy for the Future*, edited by R. Sellars, V. Mc-
Gill, and M. Farber (New York: The Macmillan Co., 1949).

and it fails to yield the certainty it is supposed to insure. In opposition to Sartre, it may be maintained that one can discover neither himself nor others in the *cogito* (Sartre holds that one discovers both himself and others therein). What may be rightly referred to as a "methodological device" should not be confused with actual reality.

The disbelief in progress, on the ground that "man is always the same," even in the face of Sartre's obvious awareness of changing social conditions and realignments of classes; the rather confused and vulgar classification of people into "cowards" and "stinkers," with respect to the alleged concealment of their "freedom"; and the vaguely expressed reference to "transcendent goals" which must be pursued by man ("man, being this state of passing-beyond"): these are further points in Sartre's lecture which indicate the woeful lack of clear and systematic thinking. Snatches of idealism are seemingly torn from the atmosphere at random, and are thrown together with insights of naturalism and even of historical materialism. Thus, Sartre asserts that "there is no universe other than a human universe, the universe of human subjectivity." Fortunately, the concept of transcendence is at hand, but it hardly suffices to pry him loose from his idealistic encumbrances. Finally, it may be observed that Sartre is simply wrong when he charges that materialism treats all men as "objects" in a narrow sense, "in no way distinguished from the ensemble of qualities and phenomena which constitute a table or chair or a stone." This opposition to materialism is seen in a still more extreme form in his essay on "Materialism and Revolution,"[58] with particular reference to dialectical materialism.

[58] "Matérialisme et Révolution," *Les Temps Modernes,* I (June–July, 1946).

IV. Additional Bibliography

1. DENMARK[59]

Anders Gemmer, *Jean-Paul Sartres Eksistentialisme* (Copenhagen, 1947).
A short critical exposition of the existentialism of Sartre.
Olof Pedersen, *Fra Kierkegaard til Sartre* (Copenhagen, 1947).
A short critical exposition of the development of existentialism from Kierkegaard to Sartre.

2. FRANCE

Les Temps Modernes, edited by Jean-Paul Sartre, Paris.
Includes articles by Sartre, de Beauvoir, Merleau-Ponty, and others.
Deucalion, edited by Jean Wahl, Paris.
Maurice Merleau-Ponty, *Phénoménologie de la perception* (Paris: Gallimard, 1945).
Robert Campbell, *Jean-Paul Sartre* (Paris: Éditions Pierre Ardent, 1947).
Henri Lefebvre, *L'existentialisme* (Paris: Éditions du Sagittaire, 1946).
Étienne Gilson, ed., *Existentialisme Chrétien: Gabriel Marcel* (Paris: "Présences," Plon, 1947).
Jean Wahl, *Petite histoire de "L'existentialisme"* (Paris: Éditions Club maintenant, 1947).
Emmanuel Mounier, *Introduction aux existentialismes* (Paris: Éditions Denoël, 1947).
Henri Mougin, *La sainte famille existentialiste* (Paris: Éditions sociales, 1947).

[59] With acknowledgment to Professor Joergen Joergensen.

George Lukács, *Existentialisme ou Marxisme?* (Paris: Les Éditions Nagel, 1948).

3. THE UNITED STATES

Philosophic Thought in France and the United States, edited by Marvin Farber (University of Buffalo Publications in Philosophy, 1950).

Contains much material on phenomenology and existentialism in both countries. Also published in France, under the title *L'activité philosophique contemporaine en France et aux États-Unis,* 2 vols. (Paris: Presses Universitaires de France, 1950).

Philosophy and Phenomenological Research, an international quarterly, edited by Marvin Farber (University of Buffalo Foundation).

Includes articles, discussions, and reviews in the fields of phenomenology and existential philosophy. H. Marcuse's discussion of Sartre's *L'Être et le Néant* and G. Stern's essay, "On the Pseudo-Concreteness of Heidegger's Philosophy," are included in VIII, no. 3 (March, 1948). A symposium on phenomenology and psychology is included in VII, no. 3.

Y. Frid, "A Philosophy of Perplexity and Indifference: Jean-Paul Sartre and Contemporary Bourgeois Individualism," trans. from the Russian by H. F. Mins, Jr., *The American Review of the Soviet Union* (New York: October, 1947).

IX

Supplements

A. Husserl on Experience and Judgment*

The claim that Husserl is still unknown, which has been
made in recent years, is based upon the extent of his unpublished manuscripts. These provide an abundance of
descriptive material, which is the real test of the value of
the phenomenological method. The present work is the
first of a series of posthumous publications and marks an
auspicious beginning in the enterprise of making available
all of Husserl's writings. It is the last part of a trilogy, the
other members of which are the now classical *Logische
Untersuchungen* and the *Formale und Transzendentale
Logik*. The latter grew out of a discussion of the meaning
of transcendental-logical problems which was originally
designed as an introduction to the present work. As Professor Landgrebe emphasizes, the *Erfahrung und Urteil*
is one of Husserl's own works, all suggestions for connecting and ordering the material having been approved by the
author himself, whose death in 1938 prevented his writing
the planned prefatory comments.

* Edmund Husserl, *Erfahrung und Urteil: Untersuchungen
zur Genealogie der Logik,* edited by Ludwig Landgrebe (1939);
discussion published in *The Journal of Philosophy* XXXVI
(1939).

The aim of *Erfahrung und Urteil* is to contribute a group of descriptive analyses for the phenomenological foundation of logic, and to continue the program of the preceding logical writings in accordance with the last period of the development of phenomenology. Formal logic is held to be in need of a process of clarification which traces back all ideas and forms encountered on higher levels of knowledge to their "origin." Logical "performance" is found to be present on all levels of experience and knowledge, not merely on the comparatively high level of linguistic statements with which the traditional logic begins. Formal logic does not inquire into the conditions of the evident givenness of the objects of judgment, and neither has psychology done so with its type of subjective examination. But the phenomenological elucidation of the genesis of judgment is interested primarily in the evident givenness of the objects of judgment as the presupposition of all judgment-evidence. The simplest case of object-evidence is that of the givenness of individuals, or of "final substrates." The theory of pre-predicative experience, which pregives the most primitive substrates in object-evidence, represents the first portion of the phenomenological theory of judgment.

The description of the nature of receptive experience shows the origin of the ideas of negation, possibility, and the modalities to lie in pre-predicative experience. The point is to show, for example, that negation is not first a matter of predicative judgment but that it already occurs in its primal form, as "annulment," in the sphere of receptivity, which is the lowest stage of the activity of the ego. Problematical possibility arises out of a situation of doubt, and is contrasted with open possibility, which is founded on the uninhibited course of perception. Abstracting from all modalizations, various stages of "perceptual performances" are described, including inner determinations of objects, or "explicatives," and "relative" determinations, referring to other objects. An attempt is also made to analyze the experience of relations on this rudimentary level. This leads to the consideration of time, which is regarded as the first and basic form, and as the presupposition of all connections which establish unity.

If the goal of cognitive activity is to be attained, it is necessary to pass beyond the domain of receptivity. The will to knowledge aims at more than the complete intuitive givenness of an object; it wants to hold fast the known once and for all. Objectivating performances of a new kind are required in order to constitute the categorial objectivities or logical structures; and since judgment is a performance of the understanding, these are called "objectivities of the understanding." This higher level of activity is characterized as a creative spontaneity which produces objects, and these are the objects which logicians have used without inquiring into the manner of their original production. So closely related are receptive experience and predicative spontaneity that every step of predication presupposes a step of receptive experience. At every stage of judgment, not only is there a further determination of the pregiven substrate, but a new kind of objectivity, the fact (*Sachverhalt*) "S is p" to mention the simplest form, is produced in creative spontaneity. Corresponding to such facts in receptivity are relationships or states of affairs, as illustrated by the relationship of larger and smaller. Facts are "discovered," and after being discovered can be thought again at will. But they were really "valid" before they were discovered.

The timelessness of the objectivities of the understanding, their "everywhere and nowhere," distinguishes them from individual objectivities. Whereas something individual has its time-place and time-duration, such an irreality as a proposition has the temporal being of supertemporality or all-temporality. By an "irreality" is meant an identical, not merely similar, determination which can occur in various realities.

The concluding section of the book is devoted to the constitution of general objectivities and the forms of general judgments. The problem is now the grasping of generalities. Such new, spontaneously produced objectivities can enter into judgments as general cores. Husserl's procedure is to ascend from the lowest and simplest empirical generalities to the highest and purest, seeking out all forms in the originalness of their production. Pure generalities are obtained by means of essential seeing (*Wesenserschauung*), and this is considered in connection with the method of variation. By freely varying a thing, an invariant remains as the necessary general form without which the thing, as an example of a species, would be unthinkable. In order to obtain a generality in a really pure form there must be no positing of reality. The general truths which refer to essential generalities are held to be prior to all truths of matters of fact in validity. Every reality that is given in experience must accordingly correspond to the *a priori* "conditions of possible experience."

Professor Landgrebe has rendered a great service in preparing so excellent an edition of this important work, which is most valuable in illustrating the nature of phenomenological analysis.

B. Major Writings of Edmund Husserl

(The works marked with an asterisk were published in the series *Husserliana* by the Husserl Archives in Louvain, under the direction of Professor H. L. Van Breda.)

Philosophie der Arithmetik (Halle: Pfeffer, 1891).

Logische Untersuchungen (Halle: Max Niemeyer, 1900–

1901). Main content included in M. Farber, *The Foundation of Phenomenology* (New York: Paine-Whitman, 1962).

Die Idee der Phänomenologie, edited by Walter Biemel (The Hague: Martinus Nijhoff, 1950).
English translation by Alston and Naknikian (The Hague: Martinus Nijhoff, 1964).

Vorlesungen zur Phänomenologie des inneren Zeitbewusstseins, written in 1905–1910, published in 1928, edited by M. Heidegger (Halle: Max Niemeyer).
English translation by J. S. Churchill (Bloomington: Indiana University Press, 1964).

Ideen zu einer reinen Phänomenologie, vol. I (Halle: Max Niemeyer, 1913).
English translation by B. Gibson (New York: The Macmillan Co., 1931).

Ideen zu einer reinen Phänomenologie, vol. I, rev. ed. by Walter Biemel (The Hague: Martinus Nijhoff, 1950); vols. II and III, edited by Marly Biemel (The Hague: Martinus Nijhoff, 1952).

Méditations Cartésiennes, translated by G. Peiffer and E. Levinas (Paris: A. Colin, 1931).

Cartesianische Meditationen und Pariser Vorträge, edited by S. Strasser (The Hague: Martinus Nijhoff, 1950).
English translation of the *Cartesian Meditations* by Dorion Cairns (The Hague: Martinus Nijhoff, 1960).
English translation of the *Paris Lectures* by Peter Koestenbaum (The Hague: Martinus Nijhoff, 1964).

Formale und transzendentale Logik (Halle: Max Niemeyer, 1929).

Erfahrung und Urteil, edited by L. Landgrebe (Prague: Academia Verlag, 1939).

*Die Krisis der europäischen Wissenschaften und die transzendentale Phänomenologie, edited by Walter Biemel (The Hague: Martinus Nijhoff, 1954).

*Erste Philosophie, edited by Rudolf Boehm (The Hague: Martinus Nijhoff, 2 vols., 1956, 1959).

*Phänomenologische Psychologie, edited by Walter Biemel (The Hague: Martinus Nijhoff, 1962).

Phenomenology and the Crisis of Philosophy, English translation by Quentin Lauer (New York: Harper & Row, 1965).

Jahrbuch für Philosophie und phänomenologische Forschung, edited by Edmund Husserl and collaborators (Halle: Max Niemeyer, 11 vols., beginning in 1913).

Index

238 INDEX

Levinas, E., 171, 233
Lewis, C. I., 22
Life-world, 41, 95
Lipps, H., 168, 193, 196
Locke, J., 70
Logocentric predicament, 29
Lotze, H., 7
Love and the world, 151ff.
Lowrie, W., 185
Lukács, G., 228
Luporini, C., 174f.

Maier, H., 120
Manheim, R., 206
Marcel, G., 161, 168f., 173, 191, 201, 203, 206, 214ff., 227
Marcuse, H., 228
Maritain, J., 164
Marty, A., 7
Marx, K., 120, 126, 158, 209, 228
Masaryk, T., 2
Massolo, A., 174f.
Materialism, 226
Maynez, E. G., 181
Mazzantini, C., 176
McGill, V. J., 47, 162, 184, 225
Mechanism and teleology, 166; and vitalism, 132f.
Meinong, A., 4, 96ff.
Merleau-Ponty, M., 94, 162, 170, 203, 227
Metaphysics, 44, 59ff., 123, 188
Methodological pluralism, 83, 183
Micu, C., 178
Mill, J. S., 6
Mins, H. Jr., 228

Misch, G., 148ff.
Modalities, 108f., 230f.
Moreno, J. E., 181
Moore, G. E., 97
Mougin, H., 227
Mounier, E., 227
Mysticism, 185

Naknikian, G., 233
Natanson, M., 47, 162
Natorp, P., 6
Naturalism, 15f., 32, 183, 226
Naville, P., 126
Nazi, 8f., 46, 157, 159, 163, 165, 185, 187f., 193, 197
Negation, 81f.
Neo-Kantian, 6
Neo-Platonic, 164
Nietzsche, F., 165f., 173, 175, 178, 189, 194, 201
Noack, H., 155
Noesis and noema, 127
Noica, C., 178
Nota, J., 196, 199

Origins, 28, 34, 40, 60, 81, 123, 230
Other egos, 58, 65

Paci, E., 175
Palagyi, M., 120
Pareyson, L., 177
Pascal, B., 178
Pastore, A., 177
Patocka, J., 162
Peano, G., 134
Pedersen, O., 227
Peiffer, G., 233

Selected titles: Revised December, 1966

hARpER ✦ tORChbOOKS

HUMANITIES AND SOCIAL SCIENCES

American Studies: General

CARL N. DEGLER, Ed.: Pivotal Interpretations of American History   TB/1240, TB/1241
A. S. EISENSTADT, Ed.: The Craft of American History: Recent Essays in American Historical Writing
    Vol. I TB/1255; Vol. II TB/1256
CHARLOTTE P. GILMAN: Women and Economics. ‡ Ed. by Carl N. Degler with an Introduction   TB/3073
MARCUS LEE HANSEN: The Atlantic Migration: 1607-1860. Edited by Arthur M. Schlesinger. Introduction by Oscar Handlin   TB/1052
JOHN HIGHAM, Ed.: The Reconstruction of American History△   TB/1068
ROBERT H. JACKSON: The Supreme Court in the American System of Government   TB/1106
LEONARD W. LEVY, Ed.: American Constitutional Law   TB/1285
RALPH BARTON PERRY: Puritanism and Democracy   TB/1138
ARNOLD ROSE: The Negro in America   TB/3048

American Studies: Colonial

BERNARD BAILYN, Ed.: The Apologia of Robert Keayne: Self-Portrait of a Puritan Merchant   TB/1201
BERNARD BAILYN: The New England Merchants in the Seventeenth Century   TB/1149
JOSEPH CHARLES: The Origins of the American Party System   TB/1049
LAWRENCE HENRY GIPSON: The Coming of the Revolution: 1763-1775. † Illus.   TB/3007
PERRY MILLER & T. H. JOHNSON, Eds.: The Puritans: A Sourcebook   Vol. I TB/1093; Vol. II TB/1094
EDMUND S. MORGAN, Ed.: The Diary of Michael Wigglesworth, 1653-1657   TB/1228
EDMUND S. MORGAN: The Puritan Family   TB/1227
RICHARD B. MORRIS: Government and Labor in Early America   TB/1244
WALLACE NOTESTEIN: The English People on the Eve of Colonization: 1603-1630. † Illus.   TB/3006

American Studies: From the Revolution to 1860

MAX BELOFF: The Debate on the American Revolution: 1761-1783   TB/1225
RAY A. BILLINGTON: The Far Western Frontier: 1830-1860. † Illus.   TB/3012
W. R. BROCK: An American Crisis: Congress and Reconstruction, 1865-57 º △   TB/1283
GEORGE DANGERFIELD: The Awakening of American Nationalism: 1815-1828. † Illus.   TB/3061
JOHN C. MILLER: Alexander Hamilton and the Growth of the New Nation   TB/3057

RICHARD B. MORRIS, Ed.: The Era of the American Revolution   TB/1180
R. B. NYE: The Cultural Life of the New Nation: 1776-1801. † Illus.   TB/3026
A. F. TYLER: Freedom's Ferment   TB/1074
LOUIS B. WRIGHT: Culture on the Moving Frontier   TB/1053

American Studies: Since the Civil War

MAX BELOFF, Ed.: The Debate on the American Revolution, 1761-1783: A Sourcebook   TB/1225
A. RUSSELL BUCHANAN: The United States and World War II. † Illus.   Vol. I TB/3044; Vol. II TB/3045
EDMUND BURKE: On the American Revolution. † Edited by Elliot Robert Barkan   TB/3068
THOMAS C. COCHRAN & WILLIAM MILLER: The Age of Enterprise: A Social History of Industrial America TB/1054
WHITNEY R. CROSS: The Burned-Over District: The Social and Intellectual History of Enthusiastic Religion in Western New York, 1800-1850   TB/1242
FOSTER RHEA DULLES: America's Rise to World Power: 1898-1954. † Illus.   TB/3021
W. A. DUNNING: Reconstruction, Political and Economic: 1865-1877   TB/1073
HAROLD U. FAULKNER: Politics, Reform and Expansion: 1890-1900. † Illus.   TB/3020
FRANCIS GRIERSON: The Valley of Shadows   TB/1246
SIDNEY HOOK: Reason, Social Myths, and Democracy   TB/1237
WILLIAM E. LEUCHTENBURG: Franklin D. Roosevelt and the New Deal: 1932-1940. † Illus.   TB/3025
JAMES MADISON: The Forging of American Federalism. Edited by Saul K. Padover   TB/1226
ROBERT GREEN MCCLOSKEY: American Conservatism in the Age of Enterprise: 1865-1910   TB/1137
ARTHUR MANN: Yankee Reformers in the Urban Age   TB/1247
GEORGE E. MOWRY: The Era of Theodore Roosevelt and the Birth of Modern America: 1900-1912 † TB/3022
R. B. NYE: Midwestern Progressive Politics   TB/1202
FRANCIS S. PHILBRICK: The Rise of the West, 1754-1830. † Illus.   TB/3067
WILLIAM PRESTON, JR.: Aliens and Dissenters: Federal Suppression of Radicals, 1903-1933   TB/1287
JACOB RIIS: The Making of an American. ‡ Edited by Roy Lubove   TB/3070
PHILIP SELZNICK: TVA and the Grass Roots: A Study in the Sociology of Formal Organization TB/1230
TIMOTHY L. SMITH: Revivalism and Social Reform: American Protestantism on the Eve of the Civil War   TB/1229
IDA M. TARBELL: The History of the Standard Oil Company. Briefer Version. ‡ Edited by David M. Chalmers   TB/3071

---

† The New American Nation Series, edited by Henry Steele Commager and Richard B. Morris.
‡ American Perspectives series, edited by Bernard Wishy and William E. Leuchtenburg.
* The Rise of Modern Europe series, edited by William L. Langer.
¶ Researches in the Social, Cultural, and Behavioral Sciences, edited by Benjamin Nelson.
§ The Library of Religion and Culture, edited by Benjamin Nelson.
Σ Harper Modern Science Series, edited by James R. Newman.
º Not for sale in Canada.
△ Not for sale in the U. K.

Myth, Symbol & Folklore

Philosophy

Political Science & Government

Psychology

Sociology

4

5